# JEANIE M. IBERLIN

## With MIKE RUYLE

# Cultivating Mindfulness in the Classroom

Foreword by ROBERT J. **MARZANO**

MARZANO
—Research—

## THE **CLASSROOM** STRATEGIES **SERIES**

555 North Morton Street
Bloomington, IN 47404
888.849.0851
FAX: 866.801.1477

email: info@marzanoresearch.com
marzanoresearch.com

Visit **marzanoresearch.com/classroomstrategies** to download the free reproducibles in this book.

Printed in the United States of America

Library of Congress Control Number: 2016958919

ISBN: 978-1-943360-09-3

*Text and Cover Designer:* Abigail Bowen

# MARZANO RESEARCH DEVELOPMENT TEAM

**Director of Content & Resources**

Julia A. Simms

**Editorial Manager**

Laurel Hecker

**Editorial Assistant / Staff Writer**

Christopher Dodson

**Marzano Research Associates**

| | |
|---|---|
| Mario Acosta | Lynne Herr |
| Tina H. Boogren | Mitzi Hoback |
| Toby Boss | Jan K. Hoegh |
| Robin J. Carey | Jeanie M. Iberlin |
| Bev Clemens | Daniel Joseph |
| Sally Corey | Bettina Kates |
| Doug Finn III | Jessica McIntyre |
| Michelle Finn | Rebecca Mestaz |
| Jane Doty Fischer | Diane E. Paynter |
| Jeff Flygare | Kristin Poage |
| Jason E. Harlacher | Cameron Rains |
| Tammy Heflebower | Tom Roy |

Mike Ruyle                              Phil Warrick

Roberta Selleck                         Kenneth C. Williams

Julia A. Simms                          David C. Yanoski

Gerry Varty

On November 1, 2014, in the early hours of the morning, I received a call that anyone would dread to hear. I held my breath as my brother told me what I already knew in my gut. My best friend and sister, Julie, had committed suicide the night before. Several weeks later as I was packing her belongings, I noticed several unopened books, CDs, and videotapes about the topics of mindfulness and meditation. In her pain, she had been reaching out for a strategy to help her ease her suffering and bring her joy. Mindfulness, as a tool to help stop negative thinking and bring about a sense of peace, had arrived too late for Julie. As an avid meditator and practitioner of mindfulness since 1994, I know that if Julie had learned these strategies earlier, she might still be alive today. I am strongly aware that mindfulness is not a cure-all, yet I am also strongly aware that mindfulness has far-reaching benefits—which this book introduces to educators for use in the classroom. Although I am not a mindfulness teacher, I have practiced intently and have served as a firsthand witness to the benefits it has provided me. This book is my gift to my sister and to children, young and old, who find life difficult. In loving memory, I dedicate this book to my sister, Julie.

—Jeanie M. Iberlin

# CONTENTS

*Reproducibles are in italics.*

CHAPTER **7** STEPS FOR IMPLEMENTING MINDFULNESS IN YOUR CLASSROOM OR SCHOOL . . . . . . . . . . . . . . . . 83

EPILOGUE . . . . . . . . . . . . . . . . . . . . . . . . . . . 97

APPENDIX A: ANSWERS TO COMPREHENSION QUESTIONS . . . . 99

APPENDIX B: NOTEWORTHY BOOKS, PROGRAMS, AND RESOURCES . . . . . . . . . . . . . . . . . . . . . 107

# ABOUT THE AUTHORS

**Jeanie M. Iberlin, EdD,** has thirty-two years of experience in education. She serves as associate superintendent of Johnson County School District in Wyoming, where she leads administrators, instructional facilitators, teachers, and other staff members in the areas of curriculum, instruction, assessment, evaluation, and professional development. Dr. Iberlin has been honored as Wyoming Assistant Superintendent of the Year for her leadership in the areas of assessment, curriculum, and instruction. She has served as a middle school principal and high school English teacher, and she has also served on several state committees. Dr. Iberlin earned an undergraduate degree from Chadron State College, a master's degree from the University of Wyoming, and a doctoral degree from Montana State University.

**Mike Ruyle, EdD,** served as a teacher, athletic coach, assistant principal, and program director in the San Francisco Bay Area and Montana for twenty-eight years. He has also been an adjunct professor and presenter at Montana State University. Dr. Ruyle created and implemented the first fully functional, performance-based model of education in Montana for the alternative program at Bozeman High School and created and led a district task force on the best practices in alternative education. His leadership in performance-based education has made him a sought-after presenter for the Office of Public Instruction, the Mass Customized Learning Summit, and numerous schools and districts throughout the Rocky Mountain region. He earned bachelor of arts degrees in history and English from the University of San Francisco and a master's degree and a doctoral degree in educational leadership from Montana State University.

# ABOUT MARZANO RESEARCH

Marzano Research is a joint venture between Solution Tree and Dr. Robert J. Marzano. Marzano Research combines Dr. Marzano's more than forty years of educational research with continuous action research in all major areas of schooling in order to provide effective and accessible instructional strategies, leadership strategies, and classroom assessment strategies that are always at the forefront of best practice. By providing such an all-inclusive research-into-practice resource center, Marzano Research provides teachers and principals with the tools they need to effect profound and immediate improvement in student achievement.

# FOREWORD

By Robert J. Marzano

*Cultivating Mindfulness in the Classroom* makes accessible to classroom teachers a set of strategies that can provide a missing foundation to the K–12 educational process. Educators have long realized that there is more to teaching than imparting new knowledge and skills in a clear and concise manner. Rather, every student sitting in every classroom is dealing with a complex internal world that involves hopes, dreams, and goals. That's the positive side of their internal worlds. The negative side includes fears, worries, regrets, and frustrations. Both sides color each student's experience at every moment of the day. When the negative parts of students' internal worlds start to outweigh the positive parts, they can be left distracted, confused, and incapable of learning. If this dynamic persists, students can slip into a negative spiral that might ultimately end in tragedy. Indeed, Dr. Iberlin's deeply personal and moving dedication at the beginning of this book demonstrates the potential consequences of ignoring these negative dynamics. Thankfully, the authors provide educators with practical tools for addressing students' internal worlds from both positive and negative perspectives. The strategies they provide all fall under the heading of mindfulness.

Jeanie M. Iberlin and Mike Ruyle begin with a solid chapter on the research underpinning their strategies. They start by surveying the research on the deleterious effects of negative attributions and emotions and end by articulating the potentially positive effects of focusing on mindfulness strategies. Next, they provide strategies for specific aspects or categories of mindfulness. They begin with stress reduction.

Stress is the hidden antagonist in everyone's life. Fortunately, there are a variety of mindfulness techniques that educators can teach students, including breathing techniques, classroom adaptations of yoga, virtual field trips, and the like. One of the more useful aspects of *Cultivating Mindfulness in the Classroom* is that it provides essential learnings for each mindfulness strategy. For example, the essential learnings for a particular breathing strategy include the following.

- Focused breathing reduces stress and instills a sense of calm.

- Doing breathing exercises once a day helps students learn to breathe from their diaphragm.

- Students can use this activity whenever they feel anxious or stressed.

Arguably, these essential learnings are as valuable as the strategies themselves because they help students gain an understanding of the connected nature of mind and body and how that connection affects their experiences moment to moment. Thus, the strategies students use in the classroom become a conduit to self-understanding and personal agency that extends far beyond the classroom.

Attention is another category of mindfulness strategies. Here, Iberlin and Ruyle begin by redefining attention as more than simply being aware of what is being presented in a particular class at a particular moment in time. Rather, attention includes being aware of the variety of types of information bombarding students throughout the day and learning to discriminate as to which of these input sources are worthy of one's focus at a particular moment in time. The authors also address the need to unplug from technology on a systematic basis to engage in a personal self-audit as to their well-being and level of awareness regarding their immediate environment.

Emotional control is another important aspect of mindfulness. The authors first address the nature and importance of emotions, noting how they can color one's thinking in positive and negative ways. Again, they provide specific techniques for emotional control, each with associated essential learnings. One of those techniques is a three-phase process of awareness, analysis, and choice. With this strategy, students can quickly and efficiently identify any situation in which negative emotions might result in skewed thinking and skewed behavior on their part. They can then determine alternative ways to think and act that would produce more favorable results. At this point, students truly have a choice in how they will act in a potentially negative situation.

Iberlin and Ruyle strongly emphasize positive self-concept as well as positive interactions with others. While we all must take care of our individual selves, we are equally responsible for taking steps to ensure that those with whom we interact benefit from those interactions in the short term and, ideally, in the long term.

*Cultivating Mindfulness in the Classroom* ends with a strong set of guidelines to implement the strategies articulated in the book. The authors emphasize the need for education on the topic of mindfulness. Teachers should continue to educate themselves about the nature and importance of mindfulness, as should leaders. Armed with this growing body of knowledge, teachers and administrations can educate students and parents as to the positive benefits of mindfulness and work to dispel any misconceptions about its intent and relatedness to the academic curriculum. Finally, the authors encourage educators to collect data to demonstrate the positive effects of mindfulness strategies and make corrections and adaptations in techniques as necessary to ensure they are meeting the needs of the students, parents, and the local community.

# INTRODUCTION

*Cultivating Mindfulness in the Classroom* is part of a series of books collectively referred to as *The Classroom Strategies Series.* This series aims to provide teachers, as well as building and district administrators, with an in-depth treatment of research-based instructional strategies that can be used in the classroom to enhance student achievement. Many of the strategies addressed in this series have been covered in other works, such as *Classroom Instruction That Works* (Marzano, Pickering, & Pollock, 2001), *Classroom Management That Works* (Marzano, 2003), *The Art and Science of Teaching* (Marzano, 2007), and *Effective Supervision* (Marzano, Frontier, & Livingston, 2011). Although those works devoted a chapter or a part of a chapter to particular strategies, *The Classroom Strategies Series* devotes an entire book to an instructional strategy or set of related strategies.

The purpose of this book is to encourage the use of mindfulness as a highly effective, low-cost strategy to help students meet their psychological needs in school and throughout life. It makes the case for why educators must help students become more mindful and offers a user-friendly approach to mindfulness that is grounded in the science of managing stress, focusing the brain for longer periods of time, and increasing emotional intelligence. *Cultivating Mindfulness in the Classroom* takes a broad view of the concept, incorporating positive psychology, emotional awareness, and a variety of pragmatic approaches.

We begin with a brief but inclusive chapter that reviews the research and theory on mindfulness. Although you may be eager to move right into those chapters that provide recommendations for practice in schools, we strongly encourage you to examine the research and theory, as they are the foundation for the entire book. Indeed, a basic purpose of *Cultivating Mindfulness in the Classroom* and others in *The Classroom Strategies Series* is to present the most useful strategies based on the strongest research and theory available.

Because research and theory can provide only a general direction for classroom practice, *Cultivating Mindfulness in the Classroom* goes one step further to translate that research into applications for mindfulness in schools. Chapters 2 through 6 describe practical strategies aligned to five major purposes and benefits of mindfulness: (1) stress reduction, (2) attention, (3) emotional control, (4) positive self-concept, and (5) positive interactions. These chapters provide detailed guidelines and activities for teachers who wish to foster these positive traits in their students. Chapter 7 presents a step-by-step process and suggestions for developing a more formal mindfulness program in a classroom or school.

## How to Use This Book

Educators can use *Cultivating Mindfulness in the Classroom* as a self-study text that provides an in-depth understanding of mindfulness practices and their effects. Each chapter explains strategies related to a beneficial component of mindfulness. As you progress through the chapters, you will also encounter comprehension questions. It is important to complete these questions and compare your answers with those in appendix A (page 99). Such interaction provides a review of the content and allows a thorough examination of your understanding. Groups or teams of teachers and administrators who wish to examine the topic of mindfulness in depth may also use *Cultivating Mindfulness in the Classroom*. When this is the case, team members should answer the questions independently and then compare their answers in small- or large-group settings.

# Chapter 1

# RESEARCH AND THEORY

Throughout the 1980s, 1990s, and early 2000s, education experienced a shift toward a focus on achievement and accountability. Few would argue against the importance of students achieving at high levels, and most would agree that some level of accountability is valuable. However, this shift also led to unforeseen changes in the content prioritized in schools. Mandated high-stakes tests, usually emphasizing English language arts and mathematics, came to the forefront, often at the expense of the arts, physical education, and social-emotional learning. Social-emotional learning in particular includes decision-making skills, self-management, self-awareness, social awareness, and people skills. Although these essential competencies are not often emphasized in schools, many teachers see the need for them, especially in the ever-changing and often stressful modern world.

## Addressing Students' Levels of Stress, Worry, and Depression

Small amounts of stress are motivating and can be positive. Excessive stress, especially in children, has negative effects on emotions and physiology (American Academy of Pediatrics, 2014). On a day-to-day basis, students feel a tremendous amount of stress. Fourteen percent of children ages eight to twelve self-reported that they worry a great deal. Forty-four percent of children and teens (ages eight to seventeen) reported worrying about success in school. Other sources of stress for eight- to twelve-year-olds include having family financial worries and getting along with their peers (American Psychological Association [APA], 2009). In a survey of 1,018 teenagers, 64 percent shared that they had felt either moderate or extreme stress in the preceding month, and 82 percent of teens said they had felt moderate or extreme stress in the preceding year (APA, 2014). Respondents also revealed the negative emotions related to their stress levels: 31 percent reported feeling overwhelmed, 30 percent reported depression, and 36 percent stated they felt fatigue. Further, findings suggested that worry and stress are impacting youth at much higher rates than perceived by parents. Only 2–5 percent of parents believed their eight-to twelve-year-olds experienced high levels of worry or stress. Youth responses indicated that they might not be receiving adequate family support to help them learn healthy strategies for handling worry and stress (APA, 2009).

In elementary school, for students who face high levels of stress, effects can include stuttering, having night terrors, crying excessively, wetting the bed, being unable to control emotions, being overly aggressive, experiencing mood swings, developing incontinence, having headaches and stomachaches, and experiencing changes in eating habits such as eating very little or overeating (American Academy of Pediatrics, 2014; Hale, 1998). Coping mechanisms for younger children can also include emotional traits such as regressing, crying, clinging, stuttering, and withdrawing (American Academy of Pediatrics, 2014).

In middle and high school students, stress can result in feelings of irritability, anger, anxiousness, and sadness. Of students surveyed, more than one-fourth reported being short or irritated with class-mates because of stress (APA, 2014). Many adolescents, when upset or distressed, react automatically, without effectively considering consequences. They can often get into the habit of using unhelpful behaviors to serve as coping strategies (APA, 2014). These include the following.

- **Over- or under-eating:** Twenty-six percent of teens reported overeating to manage stress, while 67 percent skipped meals because of a lack of appetite due to stress.

- **Not receiving adequate sleep:** Thirty-five percent of teens reported difficulty sleeping at night due to stress or worry.

- **Utilizing media to cope:** Thirty-six percent of students admitted to watching television for more than two hours a day to manage stress; 43 percent said they surfed the Internet to cope with stress; 46 percent reported playing video games to handle stress.

Stress is exhausting for students of all ages. These effects can also compound over time: "One of the most insidious effects of prolonged stress is that it pushes people into depression" (Medina, 2014, p. 67). From 2009 to 2013, the number of children diagnosed with anxiety increased by 23 percent each year and the number of children diagnosed with depression increased by 12 percent each year (Sung, 2013). The Youth Risk Behavior Survey (Centers for Disease Control and Prevention, 2013) results revealed that in the twelve months leading up to the survey, 17 percent of students seriously considered attempting suicide. Further, the same survey results showed that 28.4 percent of high school students feel sad or hopeless almost every day for two or more weeks in a row.

One source of this stress and anxiety may be technology. From iPhones to video games to texting and social media, students today are barraged with seemingly constant sensory input. While technology use has its benefits, it also has significant drawbacks. Facebook use has been shown to increase users' feelings of being socially and emotionally supported (Hampton, Goulet, Marlow, & Rainie, 2012), but overuse can have the opposite effect. A 2013 study by Ethan Kross and his colleagues studied the well-being of young adults in their late teens and early twenties in relationship to their time spent check-ing Facebook. Although the sample size was small (eighty-two participants), the results showed that the more the participants checked their Facebook accounts, the worse they felt about themselves. This type of decline in self-esteem may increase signs of depression. The connection between social media use and lowered self-esteem and signs of depression may be partially caused by incorrect impressions of other users' lives. A study (Chou & Edge, 2012) of 425 undergraduate students at Utah Valley University showed that checking Facebook is linked to the perception that other people are happier and much more successful. A study of more than a thousand Chinese teens ages thirteen to eighteen had similar findings. Teens who overused the Internet were 2.5 times more likely to experience bouts of depression than teens with normal use of the Internet (Hendrick, 2010).

Regardless of its cause, stress also interferes with students' ability to learn. When the amygdala, the brain's emotional regulator, recognizes threats or stressors, it immediately goes into fight-or-flight mode in order to keep the body safe. Unfortunately, when amygdala activity is high, the prefrontal cortex, where higher-order thinking takes place, shuts down. Too much stress causes self-protection to take over (Gregory & Kaufeldt, 2015). Thus, when there is fear, anxiety, or stress, learning opportunities decrease dramatically.

Next, we address the importance of educating the whole child, including consideration of outside stressors and other issues.

# Educating the Whole Child

Students are faced with undue amounts of stress, worry, and sensory input. These stresses are detrimental to students' emotional health and overall well-being. Combined with the shift toward emphasizing academic achievement at the expense of other skills, students' emotions and overall health have become a very distant second to the drive to achieve academically. There is no doubt that the abilities to read, comprehend, communicate ideas, and use mathematical skills are indeed essential for students. However, students also need much more from their schools.

Since the publication of *A Nation at Risk* (National Commission on Excellence in Education, 1983), followed by the No Child Left Behind Act (NCLB) of 2001 and the Every Student Succeeds Act of 2015, pressure is placed on schools to help students become college and career ready. In the past, schooling followed a one-size-fits-all model with little or no differentiation. Teachers gave students the rudiments of reading, writing, mathematics, and science and judged the students on their ability to memorize facts. Educators used this industrial-age system to give students the basic education for doing factory work, farming, or learning the family trade. As economic conditions have changed, more and more jobs have begun to require more technical skills and higher levels of education (Davis, 2016).

Under President Ronald Reagan's urgent *A Nation at Risk* message, the public was implored to improve education (National Commission on Excellence in Education, 1983). The document urged Americans to increase the rigor of education through the use of standards and higher expectations for all grade levels. High school students were required to take four years of mathematics, four years of English, and three years of science and social studies. Further, it asked that teacher education and pay be improved. This urgent plea did have some positive effects. Students completing courses in chemistry increased from 49 percent to 70 percent. Those completing geometry grew from 64 percent to 88 percent. The percentage of students graduating high school in four years rose to around 75 percent (Bohrnstedt, 2013).

The No Child Left Behind Act of 2001 demanded that schools be held more accountable. Annual report cards comparing schools' performance to other schools in each state became required. NCLB also stipulated that all students were to achieve proficiency on state tests by 2014. With this goal out of reach and with states asking for more freedom in the area of accountability, President Barack Obama signed the Every Student Succeeds Act into law in 2015. This act required states to submit annual reports to the federal government including graduation rates, student achievement data, student achievement growth statistics, and nonacademic measures such as student engagement. Despite the continued emphasis on accountability, American schools remained behind eighteen countries' educational systems in world rankings on the Programme for International Student Assessment (PISA; National Center for Education Statistics, 2012). The countries outperforming the United States in the areas of reading, mathematics, and science included Australia, Canada, China, Finland, Germany, Ireland, and Japan.

The intent on improving schools is sound. Unfortunately, the pressure on schools for their students to perform at high levels on state assessments has led to schools narrowing their focus to easily measurable outputs of basic knowledge and skills in reading and mathematics. The Center on Education Policy (CEP) conducted a 2007 study that found that between 2002 and 2007, 62 percent of schools increased instructional time for tested subjects, such as English language arts and mathematics, and 44 percent of schools decreased instructional time for subjects such as social studies, science, physical education, and art, representing an overall decrease of 31 percent. Additionally, the CEP (2007) found that schools marked "in need of improvement" under NCLB decreased students' recess time by 22 percent, an average of sixty minutes per week. Even schools that were not marked "in need of improvement," decreased their recess time by 19 percent, averaging forty-seven minutes per week (Barth, 2008). The National Academies Institute of Medicine (2013) recommended students participate in a minimum of thirty minutes of recess and physical education per school day. "Competing priorities in schools for higher test scores have resulted in physical activities of all kinds being reduced," stated Francesca Zavacky, project director for the National Association for Sport and Physical Education (NASPE). "The focus is not on the well-rounded student" (as cited in Adams, 2011, p. 56).

This is not to say that academic proficiency isn't important. It is simply not enough. As expectations regarding college and career readiness increase (as exemplified by the Next Generation Science Standards and the Common Core State Standards), students will need strong social and emotional skills (McTigue & Rimm-Kaufman, 2011). Many parents and members of the community also believe students need to develop social and emotional competencies in order to be well prepared and well adjusted (MetLife, 2002; Public Agenda, 1994, 1997, 2002). High-quality education should develop these competencies by teaching students how to have compassion for themselves and others, manage and release stress, maintain focus, make healthy decisions, build relationships, and use effective strategies for handling their emotions.

It is widely accepted that educators make a difference in students' academic achievement (Chetty, Friedman, & Rockoff, 2011; Marzano, 2007; Marzano, 2012), but highly effective educators can also have an impact on students' social and emotional learning by modeling and teaching skills such as self-awareness, self-regulation, collaboration, and decision making (Payton et al., 2008). When asked to think about the teacher who had the "most positive influence" in their life, people polled most often described this teacher as caring, personable, helpful, compassionate, and motivating (Bushaw & Lopez, 2010). Students learn most effectively when they feel safe and supported (Marzano, Scott, Boogren, & Newcomb, 2017; Payton et al., 2008; Scott & Marzano, 2014).

If students are to be prepared for and successful in their adult lives, the scope of their education must expand beyond pure academic knowledge. Including social-emotional learning in schools has the potential to help students be happier, less stressed, and more aware and in control of their emotions. Relationships and emotions have an effect on how well students learn; thus, they must become a focus for the benefit of students (Elias et al., 1997). We recommend mindfulness as a solution to these issues.

Mindfulness is a research-proven method for instilling social and emotional skills into students' and teachers' lives (Black, Milam, & Sussman, 2009; Meiklejohn et al., 2012; Rempel, 2012; Siegel, 2007). Rather than repeatedly telling students to be nice to their classmates, pay attention, quiet down, and sit still, teachers can use mindfulness to give students specific tools and practices to improve their attention, stress levels, and ability to control emotions and behaviors. Mindfulness is not a canned program, nor is it a quick fix. Rather, it is a tool that students can use throughout their lives to improve their social and emotional wellness from the inside out.

## Understanding Mindfulness

The term *mindfulness* means being consciously aware of one's own thinking and using that consciousness not only to focus on the task at hand but also to be aware of one's experience. Jon Kabat-Zinn (1994) defined mindfulness in this way: "Mindfulness means paying attention in a particular way: on purpose, in the present moment, and nonjudgmentally" (p. 4). Mindfulness gives practitioners tools to slow down and be aware of thoughts, behaviors, and actions. To better understand the meaning of mindfulness, it is helpful to look at the opposite of mindfulness—mindlessness, which can be summarized with two phrases: (1) being on autopilot and (2) going through the motions. The meaning of mindfulness, for the purpose of this book, is clear attention to what one does and thinks.

Mindfulness includes, but does not require, meditation. How one enters a meditative state can vary, but techniques to engage in mindfulness meditation often include sitting in a comfortable, yet dignified position, closing one's eyes, and focusing attention on the breath. It can encompass just a few minutes or can expand to much longer time periods. Kabat-Zinn (2005) described five core principles of mindfulness meditation.

1. A heightened awareness of internal and external experiences including thoughts, smells, feelings, the body, and sights

2. A nonjudgmental observation of these experiences

3. Compassion toward self

4. The development of openness and curiosity toward internal and external experiences

5. The ability to return to the present as thoughts arise

Awareness of breathing is often considered a core component of mindfulness. Mindfulness can also include mindful sitting, mindful walking, mindful listening, and even mindful eating. Instead of having a busy mind or constantly trying to multitask, mindfulness slows thoughts and actions, allowing for more focused attention, deeper joy, and a sense of calm.

Kristin Neff (2011), an associate professor in human development at the University of Texas at Austin, offered this tool to aid in mindfulness:

> An important tool used to develop mindfulness is the practice of noting. The idea is to make a soft mental note whenever a particular thought, emotion, or sensation arises. This helps us to become more consciously aware of what we're experiencing. If I note that I feel angry, for instance, I become consciously aware that I'm angry. If I note that my back is uncomfortable as I'm sitting at my desk, I become consciously aware of my discomfort. This then provides me with the opportunity to respond wisely to my current circumstances. Perhaps I should take a few deep breaths to calm down or stretch to relieve my back pain. The noting practice can be used in any situation and helps engender mindfulness in daily life. (p. 89)

It sounds easy. Indeed, practitioners have described mindfulness as simple but not easy. Mindfulness practice truly is simple in that it doesn't involve a lot of time, training, or expensive equipment. It doesn't cost any money. It can be done anytime, anywhere. With that being said, mindfulness has its challenges. In order to achieve the benefits, mindfulness requires disciplined, continual practice. When results are not immediately apparent, practitioners may want to forego their mindfulness practice, but inconsistent efforts limit the effects of their practice.

Mindfulness is also related to emotional intelligence, which Daniel Goleman (1995) described as five emotional and social competencies.

1. **Self-awareness:** This type of mindfulness means being aware of what one feels and using this understanding to make decisions. With self-awareness, practitioners have the ability to differentiate between subtleties in feelings such as recognizing when they are self-conscious, anxious, overly tired, irritable, or depressed.

2. **Self-regulation:** When people are mindful of their feelings, they can consider how to control their emotions so that they add to their well-being. For example, if people are

irritable, self-regulation can give them the ability to recognize they are working in a less-than-optimal state so that they can take steps to change their state or situation. One way a person could combat stress, for instance, would be to employ deep breathing exercises.

3. **Self-motivation:** This state of mindfulness enables people to set goals, have the persistence to take steps toward their goals, and eventually achieve their goals.

4. **Empathy:** This is defined as understanding how others are feeling and having rapport with diverse groups of people.

5. **Social skills:** These skills allow individuals to feel comfortable in social situations and to interact smoothly. It includes having strong people skills and knowing how to interpret the actions of others.

With all these contributing elements, it is important to have a clear delineation of what mindfulness is and what it is not for the purpose of using mindfulness in schools. Table 1.1 shows this delineation.

**Table 1.1: Mindfulness—What It Is and What It Is Not**

| Mindfulness Is | Mindfulness Is Not |
|---|---|
| • Historically based in Buddhist and Hindu practices<br>• Supported by psychological research and evidence<br>• The habit of being aware of one's own thinking and emotions in a nonjudgmental way<br>• Focused on attention to the present moment instead of rumination on the past or future<br>• A way to strengthen one's attention and focus<br>• Effective for managing stress<br>• Helpful for increasing positive feelings toward one-self and others<br>• Inclusive of many strategies and activities | • A religious practice<br>• Associated with any particular set of beliefs<br>• A spiritual or supernatural activity<br>• The same as or limited to meditation<br>• Time consuming or expensive |

In the following sections, we provide more detail regarding the background and current uses of mindfulness: its history, how it relates to psychology, and how it is recognized in mainstream culture.

## History of Mindfulness

Although this book discusses a scientific and secular approach to mindfulness, the concept does have roots in Hindu and Buddhist practices. Mindfulness is mentioned in one of the four yogic disciplines of Hinduism (Bharati, n.d.). Mindfulness is also evident in Buddhist traditions, including the five basic faculties (faith, vigor, mindfulness, concentration, and wisdom) and the eightfold path (right view, right intent, right action, right speech, right livelihood, right effort, right mindfulness, and right concentration; Brown, Creswell, & Ryan, 2015).

During the early 1900s, Americans' awareness of the term *mindfulness* began to take root. One text that helped establish the concept was *An Experiment in Mindfulness* (1958), by British Rear Admiral Ernest Henry Shattock. It shared "a way of achieving relaxed quietude in order to deal with the tension-inducing business of modern life" (Wilson, 2014, p. 30). In 1965, restrictive immigration laws were repealed and numerous Buddhists from Vietnam and Thailand moved to the United States, influencing greater acceptance of Buddhism. America's first Buddhist temple was established in Washington, DC, a year later (Wilson, 2014). In the mid-1960s, Shunryu Suzuki Roshi started the San Francisco Zen Center, which attracted young people who were trying to break free of the establishment. In 1973, Shunryu Suzuki wrote one of the best-selling spiritual books to date, *Zen Mind, Beginner's Mind* (Mukpo & Gimian, 2006). Poets, including Jack Kerouac and Gary Snyder, also helped popularize Eastern philosophies by speaking and writing about Zen enlightenment (Tomkinson, 1995). While Hindu and Buddhist introspective approaches provided the foundation for the use of mindfulness in modern science, medicine, and culture, the version of mindfulness presented in this book is both secular and research based.

Much of the credit for the mainstream and scientific acceptance of mindfulness and mindfulness meditation is due to the work of Jon Kabat-Zinn, the founder of the Stress Reduction Clinic. In 1979, Kabat-Zinn brought mindfulness to the medical realm by introducing mindfulness as a way to reduce stress, now referred to as mindfulness-based stress reduction. During his undergraduate and graduate studies at the Massachusetts Institute of Technology, Kabat-Zinn attended many Buddhist lectures. One that impacted him greatly was from Philip Kapleau, the author of *Three Pillars of Zen*. Kabat-Zinn was intrigued by the concept of learning to quiet the mind, and it greatly influenced his career (Gazella, 2005).

The term *mindfulness* was virtually unknown in American culture in the early 1970s, but the 21st century has ushered in an acceptance of mindfulness practices. In 2007, twenty million Americans meditated regularly to improve their health. In 2010, over 420 research articles were published on the topic of mindfulness (Wilson, 2014). The popularity of mindfulness has grown, in part, because of mounting evidence that it relieves stress, develops a sense of calm, and promotes happiness. Many medical doctors, psychologists, and counselors now recommend mindfulness to their clients.

## Mindfulness and Psychology

The effects of mindfulness are directly related to the way the brain and body respond to external events. External events can cause the release of neurotransmitters and hormones, two types of chemicals that are produced by and act as messengers across different systems of the body. Neurotransmitters act within the nervous system and enable communication between the neurons that make up the brain, spinal cord, and nerves. Hormones belong to the endocrine system and carry messages to organs through the bloodstream. The production of these two types of chemicals influences emotional responses and physical reactions to external events (Jensen, 2005; Sousa, 2011).

Four chemicals particularly salient to this discussion are (1) cortisol, (2) epinephrine, (3) serotonin, and (4) dopamine. Cortisol, a threat-response hormone, is released in response to stresses; it adjusts physical processes in the body, such as digestion and the immune system, for a fight-or-flight reaction. Cortisol also has an impact on cognition because of its relation to attention, emotions, and perception (Gregory & Kaufeldt, 2015; Jensen, 2005; Kuhlman, Kirschbaum, & Wolf, 2005; Sousa, 2011; Tollenaar, Elzinga, Spinhoven, & Everaerd, 2009). Because of the physiological effects they cause, long-term elevated stress and cortisol levels are associated with many mental and physical health issues, including anxiety, headaches, weight gain, and heart disease (Mayo Clinic, 2016). Epinephrine, another alerting hormone, is also involved in the fight-or-flight response to stressors—it elevates heart rate and breathing and enhances reflexes. During the fight-or-flight response, sensory input is processed primarily by the emotional centers of the brain, such as the amygdala and hippocampus, rather than by rational regions like the prefrontal cortex. In this way, stress impairs learning.

The two other chemicals are associated with more positive feelings. Serotonin and dopamine serve as calming neurotransmitters, helping to regulate our mood and attention (Ratey, 2008). Dopamine specifically is released during pleasurable or rewarding experiences, including learning. Warm and caring atmospheres can also increase levels of serotonin and dopamine in students and teachers. Wayne Dyer (2004), in his book *The Power of Intention*, described the effects of a caring atmosphere on the production of serotonin:

> The positive effect of kindness on the immune system and on the increased production of serotonin in the brain has been proven in research studies. Serotonin is a naturally occurring substance in the body that makes us feel more comfortable, peaceful, and even blissful. In fact, the role of most anti-depressants is to stimulate the production of serotonin chemically, helping to ease depression. Research has shown that a simple act of kindness . . . stimulates the production of serotonin in both the recipient of the kindness and the person extending the kindness. (p. 25)

Table 1.2 summarizes these chemicals and their functions.

**Table 1.2: Major Emotion Chemicals and Their Functions**

| Name | Type | Function |
|---|---|---|
| Cortisol | Hormone | Supplies energy; adjusts physiological processes |
| Epinephrine | Hormone | Alerts all systems; increases heart rate and breathing |
| Dopamine | Neurotransmitter | Produces pleasure |
| Serotonin | Neurotransmitter | Induces calm; regulates mood |

*Source: Adapted from Jensen, 2005, p. 72.*

These effects are even more important when one considers neuroplasticity. Neuroplasticity is the brain's ability to adapt, organize, and reorganize neural pathways from new experiences. Learning actually causes the brain to change (Diamond & Hopson, 1998; Kandel, 2006; Sousa, 2011). When an event or experience repeats, neural networks form that facilitate quicker and easier neural responses. A good metaphor for neurons wiring together is a sled sliding down a snowy hill. During the initial ride down the hill, a sled might travel at an average speed; but, if the sled follows the same path on its second run, it will travel faster because the snow has been compressed. Although the brain remains plastic throughout life, students' younger brains have greater plasticity, so it is easier to mold new and stronger patterns, including those that develop specific motor skills, informational knowledge, and emotional responses (Diamond & Hopson, 1998; Kandel, 2006; Sousa, 2011). This can be very positive for learning, as long as students are taught to practice healthy and productive habits, such as those associated with mindfulness.

The release of neurotransmitters and the brain's plasticity are also what allow mindfulness practice to have both short-term and long-lasting positive effects. When positive experiences occur, mindfulness allows practitioners to be consciously aware of and attentive to the experience. For example, as students focus their awareness on the positivity of learning, dopamine is released. The longer students can savor the positive experience through focused attention, the more the brain forms lasting connections. Neural pathways are strengthened and are more likely to fire together in future learning experiences (Lewis, 2005).

Short-term effects of mindfulness, those that are immediate, are a "combination of aliveness and centeredness" (Hanson, 2009, p. 59) and a sense of overall well-being (Grossman, Niemann, Schmidt, & Walach, 2004; Keng, Smoski, & Robins, 2011). Something as simple as taking five deep, rhythmic breaths can activate the parasympathetic nervous system, which reduces heart and breathing rates and returns the body's functions to a resting state (Divine, 2014; Hanson, 2009). One study showed a statistically significant decrease in cortisol levels in undergraduate students after only five days of meditating for twenty minutes each day. In a self-assessment, these students also reported feeling fewer depressive symptoms and decreased anxiety (Tang et al., 2007). Another short-term effect of mindfulness is the ability to be attentive to whatever thoughts arise. When thoughts are positive, mindfulness practitioners can increase the level of dopamine by being consciously tuned in to these positive feelings (Hanson, 2009). When negative thoughts arise, mindfulness teaches practitioners to consider them nonjudgmentally, without succumbing to negativity (Divine, 2014; Hanson, 2009; Keng et al., 2011). These short-term effects allow practitioners to experience a greater sense of well-being on a day-to-day basis.

Long-term effects of mindfulness, although still preliminary in research, appear to be positive as well. The longer and more dedicated the practice, the better the results. However, even small amounts of daily practice can help shape one's brain (Keng et al., 2011; Myint, Choy, Su, & Lam, 2011). Regular meditation may even increase gray matter in the cerebral cortex (Hölzel et al., 2008). The cerebral cortex, which includes the prefrontal cortex, can be likened to the CEO of the brain. Its purpose is executive functions including language, processing skills, self-regulation, memory, complex thinking, and managing multiple thoughts (Gregory & Kaufeldt, 2015). Those with more gray matter in various areas of the cerebral cortex may show higher scores on intelligence tests and increased self-regulation and flexibility in thinking (Haier, Jung, Yeo, Head, & Alkire, 2004).

While improving areas of the brain associated with executive function, mindfulness training can also decrease the size and influence of reactionary, emotional structures like the amygdala (Hölzel et al., 2008; Luders, Toga, Lepore, & Gaser, 2009). A weakened amygdala allows practitioners to be less reactive and more able to pause and make a thoughtful response. Instead of using reactionary thinking with emotions overriding the rational brain, a weakened amygdala allows for reasoned thinking where the rational mind can soothe the emotional mind (Panksepp & Biven, 2012).

Further, mindfulness has been shown to increase self-regulation abilities (Chambers, Lo, & Allen, 2008; Davidson et al., 2012; Flook & Fuligni, 2008; McKim, 2008; Ramel, Goldin, Carmona, & McQuaid, 2004). Self-regulation is the ability to manage our behaviors and feelings. It has been shown to be a predictor of student achievement in the classroom and later in the workforce (Tough, 2012). In a number of schools across the United States that utilize mindfulness training, preliminary results show improvements in students' behavior and achievement (Steinberg, 2014).

In addition to these neurological effects, mindfulness techniques have been successfully applied in various psychological and therapeutic practices. These include dialectical behavior therapy, mindfulness-based stress reduction, mindfulness-based cognitive therapy, and acceptance and commitment therapy. Marsha M. Linehan developed dialectical behavior therapy—a modified form of cognitive behavioral treatment—in the late 1970s (see Linehan, 1993). *Dialectics* refers to the synthesis or integration of opposites. The primary dialectic of dialectical behavior therapy is between the seemingly opposite strategies of acceptance and change. Thus, the components and strategies taught in dialectical behavior therapy are balanced in terms of acceptance-oriented skills (mindfulness and distress tolerance) and change-oriented skills (emotional regulation and interpersonal effectiveness).

Mindfulness-based stress reduction is an intensive treatment involving meditation practices which has been influential in introducing mindfulness to psychology. Jon Kabat-Zinn developed this model of meditative mindfulness at the University of Massachusetts Medical Center, and it has been replicated in businesses, schools, and athletic programs. Kabat-Zinn (1996) emphasized several key principles of meditative mindfulness practices.

- Making mindfulness practice something we "get to do for ourselves" as opposed to another chore we "have to do"

- Making meditation a regular habit; its greatest effects occur with regular practice

- Changing one's life habits to create the time for regular meditative practice

- Being present moment to moment; bringing an awareness to the present

- Creating a "critical mass" of supportive practitioners, which helps support ongoing commitment to the practice

- Grouping individuals heterogeneously, so participants focus on what is "right" about who they are, as opposed to limiting themselves to labels

Mindfulness-based cognitive therapy, created by Zindel Segal, Mark Williams, and John Teasdale in 1992, was designed to help clients with recurring bouts of depression. Based on Kabat-Zinn's mindfulness-based stress reduction, it encourages awareness of the present moment and disengagement from negative thinking patterns, such as those related to self-criticism or guilt. In addition to using mindfulness to reduce stress, Teasdale considered additional ways to use mindfulness-based stress reduction for his patients, including treating depression. If his patients learned to see their depression "simply as events in the mind" (Teasdale, 1999, p. 146), he surmised, they might be able to evade repeated bouts of clinical depression by examining their thoughts in a more detached manner:

> Instead of letting a bleak experience or thought kindle another episode of depression as predictably as a spark ignites a fire in bone-dry kindling, instead of allowing their feeling to drag them down into the pit of depression, patients would learn to respond with "Thoughts are not facts" or "I can watch this thought come and go without having to respond to it." (as described by Begley, 2007, p. 146)

Acceptance and commitment therapy emphasizes the importance of having a meaningful life through acceptance. As unwanted thoughts arise, acceptance and commitment therapy uses mindfulness techniques as a method for teaching clients to sit with the thoughts and gently release them (Harris, 2006). Acceptance and commitment therapy includes three categories of mindfulness: (1) being in the present moment, (2) seeing thoughts as impermanent objects, and (3) accepting what is. Further, acceptance and commitment therapy encourages observation of the self—both the thinking mind and the physical body. Evidence has shown that acceptance and commitment therapy has positive effects on varied conditions including stress, pain, post-traumatic stress disorder (PTSD), and addictions (Dahl, Wilson, & Nilsson, 2004; Twohig, Hayes, & Masuda, 2006).

### Mindfulness in Mainstream Culture

In addition to its use in psychology, mindfulness is rapidly gaining broader acceptance in mainstream culture. Prominent groups and individuals in a variety of fields have begun using mindfulness to enhance mental health, attentiveness, and productivity. The Mayo Clinic, a research group and medical practice, offers extensive mindfulness programming to more than fifty thousand employees. According to Amit Sood, the head of their mindfulness programs and a doctor in the clinic, "The human mind wanders for half to two-thirds of the day. Mindfulness is a state of mind where people are calm and relaxed, and they are in the present moment and in a state of nonjudgmental acceptance" (as cited in Hughlett, 2013). This practice helps staff members handle the stress of their roles in the clinic where they deal with life-and-death situations on a regular basis (Hughlett, 2013).

Since the 1980s, the business community has also been aware of *soft skills*, which relate to emotional intelligence and the ability to work with others. Richard Boyatzis (1982) noted that self-awareness, the ability to know one's own feelings and their effects on varied situations, distinguishes superior performers in a variety of positions, including flight attendants, business owners, psychologists, and counselors. The technology industry, too, has begun to embrace this nontraditional business practice. For example, Google has offered mindfulness training to its employees since 2007. Chade-Meng Tan, an employee at Google since 1999, brought the idea of mindfulness to the company. He was a prac-titioner of mindfulness himself and wanted to offer its benefits to other employees. In order to entice the more reluctant participants, Tan advertised it as emotional intelligence training. Thousands of employees take advantage of mindfulness training each year. The most popular mindfulness course, *Search Inside Yourself*, is taught around three core areas: (1) attention training, (2) self-knowledge and self-mastery, and (3) creating useful mental habits. This seven-week course has helped partici-pants improve their marriages, deal with grief, handle personal crises, and develop stronger self-images (Baer, 2014; Tan, Goleman, & Kabat-Zinn, 2012).

Mindfulness also has military applications. Combat tours in Afghanistan and Iraq have left many servicemen and -women facing post-traumatic stress disorder. Mindfulness offers the soldiers tools to feel more relaxed and more positive about life. In a 2011 study, 160 marines participated in extensive mindfulness training while preparing for deployment to Afghanistan. The mindfulness skills included focused attention, breath awareness, and physical awareness of the body. In addition, they learned con-crete applications and information about trauma, resiliency, and stress (Stanley, Schaldach, Kiyonaga, & Jha, 2011). After the training, the marines were exposed to an onslaught of sights, sounds, and even smells similar to what they would experience in their deployment. When compared with a control group that was not provided mindfulness training, the mindful marines showed quicker recovery in their breathing and heart rates, as well as better ability to sleep soundly without nightmares (Johnson et al., 2014; Stanley et al., 2011). A study (Jha, Stanley, Kiyonaga, Wong, & Gelfand, 2010) of a group of marines in the U.S. Marine Corps Reserve who took part in an eight-week mindfulness training prior to a stressful deployment showed an increase in working memory proportional to the time spent meditating. The control group showed a decrease in working memory, perhaps due to stress.

Sports are another area in which mindfulness has had an impact. The Seattle Seahawks, under head coach Pete Carroll, is a professional football team that has adopted a mindfulness program (Neporent, 2014). Mindfulness training is an optional offering for the players, provided by the team's sports psy-chologist, Michael Gervais. Beginners to meditation start with only a few minutes. As they become more advanced, players engage in longer periods of meditation. Mindfulness helps players be aware of their thoughts and thus better able to control them:

> By halting negative thinking and replacing it with sunnier thoughts while in training, players learn
> to carry a more positive attitude onto the gridiron. . . . This can also translate into direct physical
> advantages as well. For example, Gervais said the time players devote to sitting on a meditation

cushion with their eyes closed has taught many of them how to slow their heart rates during the intensity of play. (Neporent, 2014)

While research and scientific studies provide the true support for mindfulness, its acceptance in the mainstream can help make mindfulness training more palatable to staff, community members, parents, and students who may doubt its usefulness or question the reality of its purported benefits. Learning that mindfulness is accepted by Pete Carroll and the Seattle Seahawks may make some doubters at least curious about the practice. Knowing that Google's employees are on waiting lists to participate in mindfulness training may also add to the practice's intrigue.

## Describing the Benefits of Mindfulness

As noted throughout the previous sections, mounting scientific evidence indicates that mindfulness training benefits the brain, a person's psychological well-being, and a person's overall health. The more disciplined and regular the practice, the better the results. Even with further research needed, it is certain that mindfulness training is beneficial for practitioners. From strengthening self-control to strengthening the immune system to increasing compassion for self and others, the benefits of mindfulness closely align with what most teachers want in their classrooms: physically and psychologically healthy, focused, and engaged students who are kind to themselves and others. Table 1.3 highlights the major benefits of mindfulness and related research.

**Table 1.3: Benefits of Mindfulness and Supporting Research**

| Benefit | Sources |
|---|---|
| Emotional regulation | Chambers et al., 2008; Davidson et al., 2012; Flook & Fuligni, 2008; McKim, 2008; Ramel et al., 2004 |
| Increased focus | Panksepp & Biven, 2012; Schonert-Reichl & Lawlor, 2010 |
| Longer attention span | Black & Fernando, 2014; Panksepp & Biven, 2012 |
| Reduced rumination | Chambers et al., 2008 |
| Greater receptivity to new ideas | Moore & Malinowski, 2009; Siegel, 2007 |
| Reduced stress and anxiety | Hoffman, Sawyer, Witt, & Oh, 2010; Tang et al., 2007; Wayment, Wiist, Sullivan, & Warren, 2011 |
| Faster rebound from negative thoughts and feelings | Keng et al., 2011; Salovey & Mayer, 1995 |
| More thoughtful reactions to stimuli | Tang et al., 2007 |
| Increased compassion | Shapiro, Astin, Bishop, & Cordova, 2005; Shapiro, Brown, & Biegel, 2007 |
| Better self-control | Black & Fernando, 2014; Corcoran, Farb, Anderson, & Segal, 2010; Flook & Smalley, 2010; Siegel, 2007 |

| Less reactive | Cahn & Polich, 2006; Goldin & Gross, 2010; Ortner, Kilner, & Zelazo, 2007 |
|---|---|
| Better executive function | Flook & Smalley, 2010; Hölzel et al., 2008 |
| Increased optimism | Schonert-Reichl & Lawlor, 2010 |
| Higher working memory capacity | Chambers et al., 2008; Jha et al., 2010 |
| Improved emotional intelligence | Bridgeland, Bruce, & Hariharan, 2013 |
| Decreased depression | Siegel, 2013 |
| Better immune system | Davidson et al., 2003; Siegel, 2010 |

Although the benefits of mindfulness are many, certain benefits are particularly pertinent to the classroom educator and are worth mentioning in some detail. Improved working memory, for example, can have a major impact on students' success in the classroom. Working memory is a temporary store-house for memory where the brain consciously processes learning (Sousa, 2011). There is preliminary evidence that mindfulness training improves working memory, even in stressful situations.

Executive function is another critical attribute that can improve through mindfulness practice. Executive function helps people attend to the task at hand, recall details, manage time effectively, organize, and plan. In a school-based program of mindful awareness practices, sixty-four second- and third-grade students received thirty minutes of mindfulness training twice weekly for eight weeks. The training used breathing exercises and focused on initiating, monitoring, and shifting focus and attention. Based on questionnaires that teachers and parents filled out, students who previously had trouble with executive functioning made greater gains than those in a control group in the areas of executive functioning, metacognition, and emotional regulation (Flook & Smalley, 2010). This study showed the benefits of using mindfulness training in a school setting, especially for those students who struggle with executive functioning, and indicated that only a short amount of training is necessary (in this case, eight hours) in order to see improvements.

David S. Black and Randima Fernando (2014) studied classroom behavior of 409 students before and after a five-week mindfulness training program. The mindfulness training included three fifteen-minute sessions per week. Each week of the study focused on different aspects of mindfulness, such as breathing, body awareness, and kindness. On the days that the mindfulness teachers were not providing training, the classroom teachers spent two minutes practicing with their students. At the beginning and end of the program, teachers scored students in four areas: paying attention, self-control, participating in activities, and respect for others. Over the course of the training, the students improved in all four areas. With no more than four hours of formal training, significant improvements were reported, and the results persisted after the training had concluded.

Based on the research, as well as important concepts from various mindfulness programs, five key categories of mindfulness benefits emerge.

1. Stress reduction

2. Attention

3. Emotional control

4. Positive self-concept

5. Positive interactions

These categories are explained in detail in the following sections.

## Stress Reduction

Stress can be defined as "a relationship between the person and the environment that is appraised by the person as taxing or exceeding his or her resources and endangering his or her well-being" (Lazarus & Folkman, 1984, p. 21). Put another way, "stress is a physical, mental and emotional response to a challenging event. . . . The stress response occurs automatically when you feel threatened" (Mayo Clinic, 2014). While stress is a normal part of life, prolonged or frequent negative stress is detrimental. Stress reduction includes a set of tools or strategies that help people manage the adversities of life. It can include relaxation techniques, skills such as self-regulation, and strategies such as delineating priorities.

Practicing mindfulness helps students and adults find an inner calm. Studies have shown that mindfulness practice leads to increased gray matter in the parts of the brain that manage stress, emotions, learning, and self-awareness, which in turn leads to lower levels of stress and anxiety as well as higher levels of empathy and happiness (Hölzel et al., 2008; Schonert-Reichl, Oberle, Lawlor, Abbott, & Thomson, 2015). Further, other studies have shown promise that meditation decreases the tendency toward depression, anxiety, and anger while improving participants' overall well-being (Ricard, 2010). In an eight-week study of psychiatric patients ages fourteen to eighteen, those involved in a modified version of mindfulness-based stress reduction self-reported having reduced depression and anxiety, as well as increased sleep quality and self-esteem. The course was two hours per week and focused on three core elements: (1) attitude, (2) intention, and (3) attention. These formal practices were designed to enhance an ongoing awareness of moment-to-moment mind-body experiences, including those of a cognitive, emotional, kinesthetic, and sensory nature. Their purpose was to cultivate the capacity to be mindful during practice sessions and in daily life (Biegel, Brown, Shapiro, & Schubert, 2009).

Stress reduction is necessary for students' health and well-being. Many students routinely cope with stress caused by financial struggles in their homes, personal conflicts, pressures from the media, or lack of support in their communities (U.S. Department of Health and Human Services, 2001). Science and research have provided evidence that mindfulness can help students deal with stress in an effective manner.

## Attention

Attention focuses one's awareness on what is occurring in the present moment (*Attention*, n.d.). A more scientific definition of attention is "the ability to self-sustain mindful, conscious processing of stimuli whose repetitive, non-arousing qualities would otherwise lead to habituation and distraction to other stimuli" (Robertson, Manly, Andrade, Baddeley, & Yiend, 1997, p. 747). The ability to give one's attention requires sustained focus over a period of time (Posner & Rothbart, 1992). Sustained focus involves two processes: (1) the ability to monitor one's thoughts to determine whether or not they are focused on the task at hand and (2) the ability to adjust one's attention as needed (Malinowski, 2013). Studies have shown that mindfulness meditation increases attentional capabilities and promotes stable attention spans (Linden, 1973; Napoli, Krech, & Holley, 2005; Pagnoni & Cekic, 2007; Rani & Rao, 1996; Schmertz, Anderson, & Robins, 2009).

Studies have suggested that mindfulness and meditation practices improve attentional behaviors in children. A 1973 study showed that children ages eight to eleven who meditated had the ability to ignore distractions and focus their attention more than the children who did not practice meditation (Linden, 1973). Another study (Rani & Rao, 1996), nearly two decades later, similarly found evidence that children ages nine to eleven who regularly practiced transcendental meditation had greater attention abilities than their nonmeditating peers. A 2009 study conducted by researcher Adam Moore and psychologist Peter Malinowski examined the difference between meditators and nonmeditators in their ability to tune out distractions and focus their attention. Those who regularly meditated scored significantly higher than the nonmeditators.

Another important facet of attention is duration. This is assessed by measuring attention with a dull, repetitive task. In a study of thirty adults, researchers measured duration of attention before training in mindfulness and after participants completed a three-month practice called *shamatha* (meditation that focuses on attention). Participants focused on vertical bars and were asked to determine if they were long or short and to respond if the bar was short. Researchers required a response about a third of the time. Researchers found that the ability to attend to the dull task increased after the shamatha training (MacLean et al., 2010).

Attention is, of course, necessary for learning. Improving students' ability to focus on learning tasks will increase their ability to achieve. Attention is also foundational for cognition. A study of mindfulness training for elementary students revealed promising results from a twenty-four-week program provided to first-, second-, and third-grade students. The elementary students in this study were provided varied mindfulness training activities including mindful walking, mindful breathing, and body awareness techniques. Students practiced only two times a month for forty-five minutes during their physical education class. When compared with the control group, the participating students showed a significant increase in their ability to focus their attention and a decrease in anxiety (Napoli et al., 2005). A recent study of the effect of mindfulness practice on Graduate Record Examination (GRE) reading comprehension scores showed that students who completed a two-week mindfulness course improved their scores by 16 percent and increased their ability to attend to learning (Mrazek, Franklin, Tarchin-Phillips, Baird, & Schooler, 2013).

## Emotional Control

Mindfulness training also aids in self-regulation and emotional control. Emotional control is what people use to moderate their thoughts, actions, and emotions in response to experiences. Ross A. Thompson (1994) defined emotional regulation as "the extrinsic and intrinsic processes responsible for monitoring, evaluating, and modifying emotional reactions, especially their intensive and temporal features, to accomplish one's goals" (pp. 27–28). Self-regulation is being mindful of one's feelings and knowing one can control one's emotions and reactions so that they add to one's well-being. Research shows that mindfulness training improves emotional regulation and decreases rumination (Chambers et al., 2008; McKim, 2008; Ramel et al., 2004). Mindfulness helps people realize they can choose where to put their attention and how to react, thus giving them control in what may seem like uncontrollable situations.

A study of thirty-four students ages thirteen to eighteen, diagnosed with learning disabilities, showed significantly decreased anxiety and improved social skills after participating in mindfulness meditation for five weeks (Beauchemin, Hutchins, & Patterson, 2008). Additionally, a positive relationship was shown between mindfulness meditation and academic achievement. Teachers led the mindfulness meditation techniques for five to ten minutes at the beginning of each class period. It is promising for educators to know that mindfulness does not have to be time consuming to make a difference in students' emotional states and social interactions.

Being able to witness thoughts as they arise allows practitioners to choose a positive reaction to an unpleasant thought or feeling; mindfulness trains practitioners to quickly respond to stimuli with a controlled or objective response. Researchers Netta Weinstein, Kirk W. Brown, and Richard M. Ryan (2009) found that college students trained in mindfulness practices reacted more positively than their nonmindful peers in stressful situations. Mindfulness helped participants view thoughts, feelings, and bodily sensations as events that come and go. For example, if a student is upset about being bumped in the hallway, attention on the emotion of feeling angry can add to the student's distress. If the student is able to view the emotion of anger as an event or object that will pass, distress is lessened.

Researchers Peter Salovey, John D. Mayer, Susan Lee Goldman, Carolyn Turvey, and Tibor P. Palfai (1995) conducted a study that indicated that people with emotional clarity recovered more quickly from negative or depressing imagery than those who were less aware of their emotions. Similarly, another study had college students view picture slides associated with positive, negative, or neutral events (Arch & Craske, 2006). The study was conducted before and after mindfulness training was provided for the students. Compared to control groups, the students who had practiced mindfulness were better able to maintain a moderately positive state of being and reported feeling less emotionally volatile while viewing the various picture slides. Further, the students who practiced mindfulness had a lower level of negativity after viewing a set of extremely negative slides than either of the control groups. While we still need further research with students in grades K–12, studies such as these indicate the positive effects of mindfulness on emotional control in the general population.

Children's brains are not fully developed until age twenty-five, and the prefrontal cortex, where higher-order thinking skills, judgment, and executive functioning occur, is the last part of the brain to develop. Since students' brains are not fully formed to make strong executive decisions, it is even more critical that educators provide them with tools to increase their emotional awareness, their ability to slow down their thought processes, and their ability to consider effective choices. Mindfulness can help students step back and examine their automatic responses to situations.

## Positive Self-Concept

Positive self-concept is an individual's judgment of his or her own self-worth (Waterman, 1992). Mindfulness has been shown to benefit overall well-being and positive self-concept (Rajamaki, 2011; Rasmussen & Pidgeon, 2011; Thompson & Waltz, 2008), which can help students succeed in school. One study provided a group of high school students with instruction and twice-monthly activities designed to boost self-esteem. At the end of four years, the self-esteem group outperformed the control group in attendance, homework completion, participation in extracurricular activities, student council election, and high school graduation (Canfield, 1990).

Mindfulness likely contributes to a positive self-concept because practitioners learn to see thoughts as objects to observe and can effectively detach from negative thoughts about their self-image (Baer, Smith, Hopkins, Krietemeyer, & Toney, 2006; Pepping, O'Donovan, & Davis, 2013). A 2009 study of seventeen- to nineteen-year-old students who participated in a mindfulness training based on the Learning to BREATHE curriculum found students showed increased self-acceptance and a decrease in negative perceptions after the training (Broderick & Metz, 2009). Another study (Biegel et al., 2009) compared four- to eighteen-year-old mindfulness practitioners to a control group. After only eight weeks of training, those practicing mindfulness showed an increase in their self-esteem and a decrease in their anxiety and depression.

Students' self-concept matters, as it affects a number of essential traits, such as self-efficacy, motivation, and confidence. Self-concept also greatly affects how students present themselves, how they interpret their successes or failures, and which aspects of themselves they value (Bandura, 1994). Hattie (2012) postulated that students will often choose to act out behaviors that protect, preserve, and promote their senses of self. For example, if a student thinks of herself as the class clown, she will likely look for opportunities to act out her perceived role in the classroom. The reason people act out their self-concepts may relate to a desire for order, belonging, and self-esteem. However, one could also extrapolate from this theory that it is possible to dramatically change students' actions and attitudes by simply helping them adjust the way they view themselves. If teachers can help students learn strategies of mindfulness, students will have the tools to analyze, maintain, and shift their self-concepts as they mature. Mindfulness is a tool that, once learned, students can utilize throughout life.

## Positive Interactions

Positive interactions mean having connections and closeness in relationships, which is important for an individual's well-being. An essential part of socializing is empathizing with other humans. Evidence suggests mindfulness is an effective tool for teaching social awareness and skills (Koszycki, Benger, Shlik, & Bradwejn, 2007; Kocovski, Fleming, & Rector, 2009). According to psychologists Randye Semple, Jennifer Lee, and Lisa Miller (2006), mindfulness works in this manner:

> By experiencing thoughts, emotions, and sensations as independent of external events, a practitioner of mindfulness can more easily "decenter" from anxious, previously conditioned, internal experiences. Through repeated personal experiences we begin to perceive our thoughts, emotions, and sensations as transient, continually shifting events in the mind rather than evidence of objective truths. (p. 149)

Mindfulness promotes connections and closeness in relationships (Kabat-Zinn, 1994; Welwood, 1996). Since mindfulness promotes receptivity, practitioners are more aware of others' communication, emotions, and thoughts (Kemeny et al., 2012). Ruth Baer (2014) found that mindfulness correlates to emotional intelligence, which includes social skills and perspective taking. Research also supports mindfulness as effective in reducing social anxieties (Dalrymple & Herbert, 2007; Kocovski et al., 2009).

Strong social and emotional skills are essential for being a good student, friend, and family member, and can help students succeed in college and in their careers. Mindfulness training can provide students with tools for developing and fine-tuning their interactions with others.

## Translating Research and Theory Into Practice

Throughout their time in K–12 education, students progress through critical stages of development in which they establish habits and learn skills that will promote their health and well-being in the present and throughout their adult lives. Research shows that integrating social and emotional learning aids students in achieving at higher levels by giving them essential life skills, including the ability to focus for longer periods of time, interact positively with peers and adults, and persist with grit and tenacity. Empirical evidence also indicates that mindfulness promotes psychological health and well-being. Providing students with the tools of mindfulness has the potential to improve their interpersonal relationships, self-esteem, academic achievement, and physical and mental health. The remaining chapters build on the research and theory presented here to provide details on how to incorporate mindfulness into schools and classrooms. Each chapter focuses on one of the five key categories of benefits: (1) stress reduction, (2) attention, (3) emotional control, (4) positive self-concept, and (5) positive interactions. Along with a description of why mindfulness works, each chapter provides practical tools for educators to use with students. As mentioned in the introduction, each chapter also includes comprehension questions to help readers process the content. After completing each set of questions, readers can compare their answers with those in appendix A (page 99).

# Chapter 2

# STRESS REDUCTION

One of the most important and well-documented benefits of mindfulness is stress reduction. Mindfulness is not about doing things perfectly or never feeling anxiety; however, it can help people notice and respond to stress in ways that restore a healthier, happier state of being. For students, and for educators, life can sometimes feel overwhelming. As noted, research has shown that students of all ages are feeling exhausted, depressed, irritable, and overwhelmed in their everyday lives (U.S. Department of Health and Human Services, 2001; Weissberg, Walberg, O'Brien, & Kuster, 2003). The human body is conditioned to handle danger and stress; the fight-or-flight response primes the body to protect itself. However, frequent or prolonged periods of this response take a toll on one's health and well-being. Relaxing is the opposite of the fight-or-flight response; it decreases heart rate and blood pressure and increases attention and cognitive function (Benson, 2010). Mindfulness offers students and teachers specific techniques to reduce stress, relax, replenish, and re-energize.

This chapter offers several tools to reduce stress and induce a feeling of relaxation. Teachers can introduce and practice these tools with students. Some students will respond better to certain activities—mindfulness is not a one-size-fits-all strategy—so teachers can encourage students to regularly practice the ones that make them feel calm and relaxed. The key to maximally reaping the benefits of these techniques is to practice them regularly until they become as natural to students as brushing their teeth, something most people would never go a day without doing. Here, we will discuss stress-reducing strategies related to (1) deep breathing, (2) silence, (3) yoga, and (4) field trips.

## Deep Breathing

Many people have heard the popular adage that they should take a deep breath and count to ten to reduce feelings of stress or anger. Mindfulness training takes this method a step further; it encourages practitioners to pause, notice their feelings, take a deep breath, and have a more thoughtful response to the event or experience. Deep breathing relaxes the body, slows the heart rate, and decreases stress and anxiety. The brain requires oxygen to operate effectively. Breathing increases oxygen in the bloodstream, thus fueling the brain. Deep breathing is one of the simplest methods available to become more mindful, and students can use it anytime, anywhere. Thich Nhat Hanh (2015), a Zen monk, described mindful breathing in this manner:

> We follow our in-breath and our out-breath, making space for silence. We say to ourselves, "Breathing in, I know I'm breathing in." Breathing in and out mindfully, paying attention only to the breath, we can quiet all the noise within us—the chattering about the past, the future, and the longing for something more. (p. 5)

Asking students to take a few deep breaths is an easy brain break for educators to use regularly or when the class's attention is waning. Encourage students to truly feel the breath, starting with the inhale through the nose. Ask them to be present with this sensation. Then encourage them to watch their bellies rise as they intake the air. Have them feel the sensation as they push the air back out. Deep breathing is surprisingly both calming and invigorating and can help students stay focused and alert for effective learning.

In addition, we detail two specific breathing activities teachers can use with their students: (1) box breathing and (2) breathing buddies.

## Box Breathing

Box breathing is an easy-to-understand, simple-to-do exercise that uses a visual cue to help students practice deep, mindful breathing (Divine, 2014). Regular use of this breathing technique makes deep breathing more natural and accessible. Further, it provides a tool for students to use during emotionally challenging situations. Once taught to students, this activity can become part of a daily or systematic practice. When students begin the day, they can use box breathing to help them release the stress of their morning and prepare for the day ahead. After recess, teachers can help elementary school students settle back into the rhythm of learning by initiating a few focused minutes of breathing. Middle and high school teachers can also systematically begin their classes with box breathing. Investing time in this technique during transitions or at the beginning of class reaps rewards during critical learning time. Box breathing is appropriate for students in grades K–12.

Here, we'll discuss three important elements to consider in regard to box breathing: (1) preparation, (2) essential learnings, and (3) directions.

### *Preparation*

To get ready to lead this practice, teachers should consider practicing box breathing for several weeks. It is an easy discipline to adopt. In fact, noticing boxes or rectangular shapes in daily life can serve as a reminder to pause for a few deep diaphragmatic breaths. For example, while driving to work and stopping at a red light, the windshield's shape can serve as a reminder to take a deep breath.

When implementing this activity in class, teachers need only allot three to five minutes. No materials are required, but teachers might choose to draw or display a box shape on the board to help students visualize the directions (see figure 2.1).

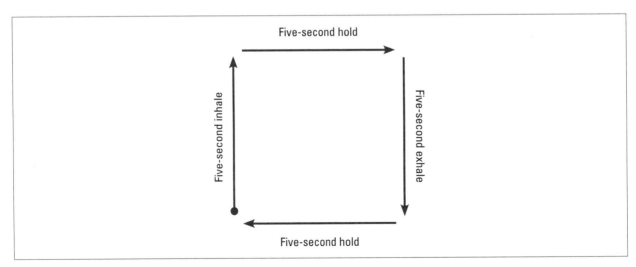

**Figure 2.1: Box breathing diagram.**

### *Essential Learnings*

In order to help students understand the purpose of box breathing and get the most benefit from the activity, teachers should directly teach the following points.

- Focused breathing reduces stress and instills a sense of calm.

- Doing breathing exercises once a day helps people learn how to breathe from their diaphragm.

- Students can use this activity whenever they feel anxious or stressed.

### *Directions*

Teachers can guide students through box breathing using the following six steps.

1. Instruct students to sit comfortably in a chair or on the floor.

2. Begin by telling students to look at or imagine the box shape and exhale completely. Start at the lower left corner of the box and prompt students to inhale for five seconds as you move up the left side of the box.

3. As you move along the top of the box, hold for five seconds.

4. As you move down the right side, exhale for five seconds.

5. As you move along the bottom of the box, hold for five seconds.

6. When you arrive back at the beginning, repeat.

Teachers can either count out loud or use a pointer to silently indicate the pace, which they can modify as appropriate for students. For example, elementary school students might need to do box breathing in intervals of three seconds due to their smaller lungs.

## Breathing Buddies

Teachers of students in the primary grades may want to try breathing buddies (Goleman, 2013) as an introductory mindfulness activity. Young children face many stressors but often lack adequate tools to help manage them. This activity involves having students practice deep breathing while holding onto a stuffed animal. Holding onto a comforting and familiar toy can soothe them as they learn to use their breath as a relaxation tool. To adapt this activity for older students, teachers can ask them to bring in a meaningful object to hold, such as a special pillow, a photograph, or something related to a favorite activity.

Breathing buddies is a perfect way to set the tone for the day. It is easy to do and helps educators create a warm, caring environment and get students ready for learning. Teachers can establish a routine for this mindfulness activity by inviting students to get their breathing buddy as soon as they enter the classroom and to head to the carpet or other designated area. Then, during this quiet time, teachers can take roll, answer questions from students or parents, and begin the day with a calm classroom. Another perfect opportunity for breathing buddies is after recess. While physical activity is beneficial for learning, the transition from the high energy of recess back to the classroom can be challenging. Breathing buddies can help students relax and prepare for learning. Breathing buddies is most appropriate for grades K–2, but teachers can adapt it for all ages.

Here, we discuss three important elements to consider with this activity: (1) preparation, (2) essential learnings, and (3) directions.

### Preparation

This activity requires that each student have a stuffed animal. As such, some advance planning is required. Teachers can invite students to bring in a stuffed animal from home, but must also prepare for students who do not have one to bring. Teachers should equip the classroom with several spare stuffed animals if teachers use this method. Alternatively, the teacher could have a classroom set of stuffed animals—enough for every student. Teachers can also play soothing music during this activity if they wish.

### Essential Learnings

Explaining points such as the following to students can help them better understand the activity and why it is important.

- Deep breathing can help people relax and get ready to learn.

- Quiet time can be very nice.

### Directions

Breathing Buddies involves the following four steps.

1. Students retrieve stuffed animals and hold them in their laps.

2. Explain to students how to do a deep belly breath. One way is to pretend they are taking in air through a straw. Ask them to watch their bellies rise as the air comes in.

3. Label this as a *deep belly breath*.

4. Students then follow a teacher-led pattern for deep belly breathing, such as inhaling for three counts and exhaling for three counts. Repeat this five to ten times. As students develop more breathing stamina, teachers can extend this time to three to five minutes.

## Silence

In the busyness of day-to-day life, the average person rarely experiences intentional, focused silence. Noise has been shown to have negative effects on students' health, well-being, and achievement (Novotney, 2011). Further, taking time for quiet moments can help alleviate stress and improve well-being (Goldstein, 2007). Mindfulness can help students ease into being comfortable with silence. By experiencing moments of silence, people are more able to notice the subtlest of sounds—birdsong, a child's laughter, the honking of a horn in the distance, or the sound of a mindfulness chime. Each one of these sounds, when given one's attention, can serve as reminders to listen mindfully, to be aware, to be present, to notice. Teachers can encourage students to try mindful silence by suggesting scenarios in which they can perform this practice. For example, instead of automatically listening to music when they get in the car, students can try driving or riding to school without any music. Additionally, instead of constantly trying to be in the company of others, have them consider taking some time to be alone. Encourage students to take time for silent reflection each day. In addition, the following sections describe two specific activities to this end: (1) Seeking Silence and (2) glitter jars.

### Seeking Silence

Seeking Silence is a journaling activity that encourages students to include purposeful silence in their days. They can use this activity as an opportunity to set goals and reflect. Seeking Silence is appropriate for grades 3–12. As with the previous two activities, consider the same three elements: (1) preparation, (2) essential learnings, and (3) directions.

### Preparation

This activity requires only paper and writing utensils. However, it takes place over two sessions, so teachers should schedule fifteen to thirty minutes for this activity at two different times and create a plan to make sure students do not lose their journal entries between sessions. If students have academic notebooks or journals that are kept in the classroom, they can write their seeking silence entries alongside other notes. Teachers can also collect the entries at the end of the first session and redistribute them for the second session.

### Essential Learnings

Teachers should discuss this important background information with students during the first session of this activity.

- Silence is a powerful stress reducer. Silence induces a sense of tranquility and calm.

- It is possible to incorporate silence into many daily activities, such as walking, eating, showering, and so on.

### Directions

Teachers can use the following five steps to lead this activity in their classrooms.

1.  Provide students with the essential learnings. Lead a discussion about times when they have experienced moments of peaceful stillness. Is it common or rare in their lives and why?

2.  Invite students to consider a noisy time of day when introducing stillness would help them. Ask them to journal about how they think silence could help.

3.  Elicit students to share their thoughts, if they wish. Then invite them to write a goal related to silence. For example, instead of watching television while falling asleep, a student might set a goal to avoid noise and distractions during bedtime at least twice a week.

4.  After students write their silence goal, have them anticipate any obstacles that may get in their way. As they journal, invite them to come up with solutions to overcoming the obstacle. For example, one obstacle may be a best friend always texting at a certain time. One solution for this obstacle may be to let that friend know about the silence goal.

5.  Set a follow-up discussion time for a few days later. Invite students to share their successes or attempts. Lead them in a discussion of what may have worked or failed in trying to add more silence into their day.

## Glitter Jars

In addition to external noise and stimuli, the mind itself can interrupt silence with nonstop thinking. Nonstop thinking is when the mind is continually occupied with thoughts, emotions, and worries. Teachers can demonstrate a powerful metaphor for how a student might feel while managing the constant stimuli of everyday life by asking the student to picture a snow globe she has recently shaken. The flurries swirl around, dominating and obscuring the scene. Students may feel that a barrage of thoughts and feelings—as chaotic as the snow in a snow globe—dominates their minds on a day-to-day basis.

But, just as the snow in a snow globe eventually settles down to the bottom, students can learn techniques to reduce nonstop thinking and create a clear mind. This activity (Willard, 2010) helps students visualize this concept by having them create their own snow globes or glitter jars. Teachers can model and reference this project as a metaphor for minds that are constantly processing information and use it to launch a discussion of tools that calm the mind, such as box breathing and Seeking Silence. This activity is appropriate for students of all ages.

### Preparation

This activity can take twenty to forty minutes. If this activity is done as a demonstration, a teacher will need one canning jar, baby food jar, or other glass or clear plastic jar with a watertight lid. If students are to make their own glitter jars, each student or small group of students will need a jar. Various colors of glitter can represent different thoughts and feelings. Each jar will also need to be filled with water, so teachers should make water available to students.

### Essential Learnings

Teachers can use the following key points to explain the snow globe metaphor and provide context for this activity.

- The mind is similar to a snow globe. At times, it is settled and calm. Other times, it is filled with flurries. People have tools to help them calm the flurries.

- The jar is similar to a person's mind. Each color of glitter represents a thought or feeling that person has.

- People do not need their thoughts and feelings to go away. They just need thoughts to settle down so they can see clearly.

### Directions

Teachers can follow these nine steps to create glitter jars with students.

1. Fill the jar with water. Ask students to name some thoughts that seem to swirl around in their minds. Some examples may include worrying about grades, dealing with friendship issues, missing a free throw in a basketball game, obtaining troubling information from the news or media, and so on.

2. Add some glitter of one color to represent one thought—for example, "Blue represents when we worry about who we will sit with at lunch." Swirl it slightly.

3. Add another color to represent another thought or feeling, such as, "Green represents what is going on in the media." Swirl it slightly.

4. Continue this process with three or four different colors.

5. Seal the jar by fastening the lid tightly.

6. Show the students that at times the thoughts and feelings are very calm, such as when they first get up in the morning. All of the glitter will be at the bottom of the jar during this explanation.

7. Begin to shake the jar while describing events that might cause their thoughts to grow louder throughout the day. For example, perhaps the student was late for school and dropped some books on the way to class. Maybe someone wrote something mean on the

student's locker, or a new friend smiled at the student. Ask students to notice how the glitter starts swirling as these thoughts compound.

8. Invite students to discuss how to make the water clear again. Their answers may include stillness, silence, deep breathing, meditation, and so on.

9. Share the essential learnings with the students: We do not want our thoughts and feelings to go away. We just want them to settle down so we can see clearly.

## Yoga

Yoga, although a popular trend, has been around for a long time. It is a Sanskrit word which means to "'yoke,' or unite, the mind, body, and spirit" (KidsHealth, 2016). The goals of yoga are gaining physical strength and agility as well as finding balance in life.

Mindfulness skeptics often accept yoga more than practices such as meditation, perhaps because the stress-reducing effects of physical activity are well known. Yoga has tremendous physical benefits, including improved balance, flexibility, and muscle strength, as well as lowered blood pressure and stress levels (Noggle, Steiner, Minami, & Khalsa, 2012). Yoga poses also incorporate breath awareness as part of the practice. In a preliminary study published in the *Journal of Developmental and Behavioral Pediatrics*, high school juniors and seniors participating in yoga showed less anxiety and better moods than a control group (Noggle et al., 2012). Here, we introduce three beginner poses appropriate for all ages: (1) Sunrise Pose, (2) Tree Pose, and (3) Downward Dog. Before each pose, have the students take a thirty-second stretch break (if needed).

### Sunrise Pose

This pose is a quick, simple stretch that teachers can utilize anytime throughout the day (Buckley, 2003). Again, please consider the following three elements: (1) preparation, (2) essential learnings, and (3) directions.

#### Preparation

At times throughout the day, students' energy may be lagging or their attention unfocused. Students can do yoga poses in a small space and in as few as three to five minutes. Teachers will want to ask students to spread out in the classroom and be mindful of others' space. Students can do the Sunrise Pose to refocus.

#### Essential Learnings

Note these facts about yoga.

- It is important to give our brains breaks occasionally throughout the day. One way to do this is through yoga.

- The goals of yoga are to gain physical strength, flexibility, and balance, and to reduce stress.

- It can be accomplished in a very short amount of time.

- Yoga has been around for thousands of years.

#### Directions

Consider the following five steps.

1. Invite students to stand tall and proud.

2. Ask students to take four deep belly breaths.

3. On the fourth inhale, instruct students to lift their arms straight above their heads.

4. Have students stretch their arms, spines, and waists toward the sky, and press their legs and feet down toward the ground. Hold for five seconds (see figure 2.2).

5. Relax.

**Figure 2.2: Sunrise Pose.**

## Tree Pose

This is a classic pose that helps students develop body awareness and balance. Students of all ages enjoy the challenge of trying to balance on one leg.

### Preparation

Students can accomplish the Tree Pose in just a few minutes. They will need space to be comfortable and not too close to other students.

### Essential Learnings

Consider these facts about the Tree Pose.

- This posture improves physical balance, calms the mind, and improves the ability to focus while strengthening our core and leg muscles.

- We can imagine that the stillness and balance of our bodies reflect the calmness and stability of our minds.

### Directions

Consider the following five steps.

1. Instruct students to stand on one foot.

2. Tell them to imagine that foot attaching to the floor like a tree trunk with roots anchoring it.

3. Next, students bring the other foot up and rest it on the standing leg just above the knee.

4. Students raise both arms out to the side or above their heads like tree branches, strong and firm. They can also clasp their hands in front of their chest if it helps them balance (see figure 2.3).

5. Repeat on the other leg.

**Figure 2.3: Tree Pose.**

For variations, ask students to wave their arms like tree branches in the wind. This challenges students' balancing efforts. Additionally, students can try closing their eyes while maintaining their balance.

## Downward Dog

This is an energizing pose that strengthens muscles, changes a person's perspective, and aids in flexibility. Elementary school students can imagine they are dogs or wolves or coyotes while doing this pose. As with other activities, consider the same three elements: (1) preparation, (2) essential learnings, and (3) directions.

### *Preparation*

This particular pose takes up more room than other poses. Students will need adequate space for kneeling on all fours and stretching without bumping into others. It is important to remind students to be aware of other students' space.

### *Essential Learnings*

Consider these facts about Downward Dog.

- Downward Dog is one of the most well-known and essential yoga positions.

- It increases flexibility while strengthening the body.

- One key to doing this move correctly is to keep your weight mostly on your feet.
- If students aren't as flexible, it is okay for them to bend their knees. Flexibility will improve over time.

### *Directions*

Consider the following seven steps.

1. Have students start out kneeling on all fours.
2. Tell students to spread their fingers and press their palms into the floor.
3. Next, have them straighten their legs and push their hips into the air, making an upside-down V shape (see figure 2.4).
4. Remind students to relax their neck muscles.
5. Tell them to look between their legs for a new perspective.
6. Ask students to walk their hands slowly back toward their feet into a hamstring stretch. Hold the stretch for five seconds while breathing deeply.
7. Gently unroll the spine and return to standing.

**Figure 2.4: Downward Dog.**

## Thirty-Second Stretch Break

When short on time, a thirty-second stretch break helps students focus for upcoming learning. Teachers can use it several times a day if needed.

### *Preparation*

This is an activity that teachers can use as needed throughout the day. As energy levels lag, teachers can invite students to participate in a stretch break. Once the class is familiar with the process, various students can lead the stretch break.

### *Essential Learnings*

Note the importance and usefulness of stretch breaks.

- Our brains need oxygen to learn effectively. Oxygen is fuel to our brains.

- A simple stretch break increases our oxygen levels. This helps us focus and stay alert for learning.

- Sometimes learning or creative ideas occur while we are moving.

### Directions

Consider the following seven steps.

1. Instruct students to stand up and shake their arms out.

2. Have students stretch their arms up high toward the sky. Let them know it's okay to make stretching noises, such as "mmm" or "ahh."

3. Ask students to lower their arms back to their sides.

4. Tell students to tilt their heads gently to the left, roll their heads gently to the front, and then over to the right and back to the center. Repeat in the opposite direction.

5. Have students roll their shoulders to the back four times.

6. Have students roll their shoulders forward four times.

7. Finally, ask them to shake their arms out one last time and be seated.

## Field Trips

Sometimes the best way to reduce stress is to go to a relaxing location. While planned all-day or half-day educational field trips can be an occasional welcome break for students, the mini field trips we suggest here are intended as short, more impromptu excursions that allow students to get away from the classroom briefly, whether physically or in their imaginations. The following sections describe two strategies: (1) virtual field trips and (2) nature walks.

### Virtual Field Trips

Even when unable to physically travel, people can use their imaginations to take a virtual field trip. Many students will know of a peaceful place that they can recall when prompted. Other students will need more guidance to remember or imagine one. Teachers can use the following activity to evoke a sense of relaxation in a short period of time. It also is a powerful tool students of all ages can use any time they feel tense. Again, consider the following three elements: (1) preparation, (2) essential learnings, and (3) directions.

#### Preparation

This activity does not require any materials and only takes five to ten minutes.

#### Essential Learnings

The following points can help students understand the purpose of this activity.

- By recalling a peaceful place in their minds, people can access that same sense of calm without actually being there.

- Everyone can access calmness through practice. The more one practices it, the easier it is.

### *Directions*

Teachers can use the following eight-step script or one of their own creation to guide students on a virtual field trip.

1. "We are about to go on a field trip. It's a virtual field trip, so no need to bring anything except your imagination."

2. "Breathe in three deep belly breaths. Feel yourself relaxing. Feel the stress leaving your neck and shoulders. Feel your jaw relax. Relax your eyes."

3. "If you feel comfortable doing so, allow your eyes to close."

4. "Think of a place where you can picture yourself feeling peaceful and calm. Maybe you've been there already. Maybe it's a place you'd like to visit. Maybe it's your couch or lawn chair. Maybe it's the ocean or a mountain scene. See yourself there now."

5. "Enjoy your virtual field trip to this peaceful place. Drink in the colors and the sounds."

6. "Breathe in all of the sights, sounds, and textures for several deep breaths."

7. "Feel tension leaving your body as you relax into your peaceful place."

8. "When you are ready to return to the classroom, please open your eyes and rejoin us."

## Nature Walks

One of the easiest ways to help students relax is by taking them into nature. Many people seek out natural environments to reduce stress. Research shows that interaction with nature positively impacts stress levels and quality of life (Grinde & Patil, 2009). Patients in hospitals with views of green spaces heal more quickly than those without (Franklin, 2012; Ulrich, 1984). In a study of public housing buildings, buildings with greater amounts of vegetation and green space had 52 percent fewer crimes than buildings with less vegetation and green space (Kuo & Sullivan, 2001).

Nature walks, as described in this section, can last as little as fifteen minutes. Use this activity as often as time allows. It is especially useful as a soothing strategy when students are tense about an event such as state testing or when they are unusually restless. To use this activity in a more urban setting, encourage students to look for signs of nature such as trees, flowers, soil, birds, the color of the sky, and the shape of the clouds, as well as to be especially mindful of colors, sounds, and shapes. Nature walks are appropriate for students in grades K–12. Consider the following three elements with regard to nature walks: (1) preparation, (2) essential learnings, and (3) directions.

### *Preparation*

Students can accomplish this activity in fifteen to twenty-five minutes. They will need appropriate clothing for the weather and, optionally, journals and pens for journaling during or after the nature walk.

### *Essential Learnings*

Teachers can explain the following points to students to help them understand the benefits of spending time in nature.

- Being in nature is calming and soothes the nervous system.

- Research supports the use of nature for healing. Patients in hospitals with views of green spaces heal more quickly than those without (Franklin, 2012).

### Directions

The following six steps may be useful for teachers who wish to implement nature walks with their students.

1. Take students outdoors and ask them to gather around you. Share with them that this is a mindful nature walk for the purpose of enjoying the outdoors. Remind them of safety and staying together as a group.

2. Encourage them to conduct the nature walk without talking.

3. Ask them to move at a calm, leisurely pace while noticing the sights, sounds, and textures in nature.

4. With each mindful step, encourage students to notice the ground beneath their feet supporting them.

5. With each mindful breath and each mindful exhalation, encourage students to notice the fresh air filling their lungs.

6. When the students return to the classroom, you may want to offer them time to capture their experience in writing. A possible prompt for their writing could include the following: "Free write about your nature walk. What colors stood out to you? What sounds did you notice? What textures did you touch?"

## Summary

Life seems to be more stressful now for students than ever before. They must manage stresses associated with school, home, and friendships. In the face of challenging events and situations, teachers can provide students with mindfulness tools that help them access a state of inner calm and relaxation. In this chapter, we introduced several stress-reduction tools, including breathing exercises, yoga, field trips, and silence strategies. The next chapter addresses maintaining focus and paying attention—two cognitive skills that students can develop through mindfulness and closely relate to stress reduction. We provide tools and describe processes in the following chapter that can help students focus and give their attention to the present moment.

# Chapter 2: Comprehension Questions

1. How does stress negatively impact the body?

2. Why are breathing exercises useful in the classroom?

3. How does the glitter jar activity help students visualize nonstop thinking?

4. According to research, what positive effects does nature have on people?

# Chapter 3

# ATTENTION

Another key aspect of mindfulness is attention—focusing on the present and the task at hand. Staying present and attentive helps people concentrate on and be more successful in various tasks and interactions. Even during seemingly ordinary or mundane tasks, such as making one's bed in the morning, showering, or riding to and from school or work, it is possible to remain present, engaged, and consciously aware of each moment. Although intentionally letting one's mind wander can be beneficial for creative purposes, many people may notice that their minds wander unintentionally. Most people have experienced arriving at a familiar location with no recollection of the drive there or reading pages in a book without retaining any of the information. These are examples of automaticity, the opposite of mindfulness or presence. Presence has been likened to the term *flow* (Csikszentmihalyi, 1990), which describes a state in which one is immersed in the here and now, and fully focused on the task, event, or interaction at hand.

Josho Pat Phelan (2010) described mindful attention through the lens of washing dishes:

> You will not have to stop and ask yourself: "Are my hands in the water or out?" "Does the water feel hot or just lukewarm?" . . . When we wash dishes we know directly and immediately the heat and sudsy quality of the water without needing to pull ourselves back from the situation to think about it. . . . Once we step back to examine an experience, the original experience has ended and we begin . . . reflecting on the past. (pp. 132–133)

People often think this type of mindfulness would be exhausting, but mindful attention can be relaxing. However, this type of sustained attention requires practice: "Attention is a skill just as playing piano is. We'd never get upset with a student who played piano poorly if we never taught the student how" (Rechtschaffen & Rechtschaffen, 2015). With focus on presence, one can strengthen and develop this ability over time.

The brain takes in a tremendous amount of stimuli through the five senses. Of course, it is not possible to focus on all of the external stimuli that the brain absorbs, but teachers can help students be more purposely attentive. Purposeful attentiveness leads to a higher level of engagement and cultivates the ability to focus for long periods of time. Presence is also fundamental to one's overall well-being and capacity to handle distressing situations. Ellen Langer (2014), a research scientist and professor at Harvard University, expressed the importance of trying to be mindfully present at all times:

> Trying to remain mindful in all that we do may seem exhausting. In many talks I've given over the years, people shudder when I say we should be mindful virtually all the time. They think it's hard work. I believe that being mindful is not hard, but rather it may seem hard because of the

anxious self-evaluation that we add. "What if I can't figure it out?" Anxiety causes stress, and stress is exhausting. Mindfulness is not. Being mindful allows us to be joyfully engaged in what we are doing. (pp. xxii–xxiii)

It is also important for educators to be aware that students' ability to attend to learning varies. There are many reasons for this, including culture, desensitization to stimuli, illness, and anxiety levels, to name a few. Table 3.1 depicts the varied tendencies people can have, which have a direct impact on learning.

**Table 3.1: Aspects of Attention and Tendencies**

| Tendency Regarding Level of Attention | Aspect of Attention | | |
|---|---|---|---|
| | **Holding Onto Information** | **Updating Awareness** | **Seeking Stimulation** |
| **High** | Obsessiveness<br>Overfocusing | Porous filters<br>Distractibility<br>Sensory overload | Hyperactivity<br>Thrill-seeking |
| **Moderate** | Good concentration<br>Ability to divide attention | Mental flexibility<br>Assimilation<br>Accommodation | Enthusiasm<br>Adaptability |
| **Low** | Concentration fatigue<br>Small working memory | Fixed views<br>Obliviousness<br>Flat learning curve | Stuckness<br>Apathy<br>Lethargy |

*Source: Hanson, 2009, p. 181.*

Students with moderate levels of attention can generally concentrate on tasks with ease and may be perceived as having ideal levels of focus. Highly attentive students tend to overfocus, which may cause stress and interfere with their learning. On the opposite end, students with low attention tendencies may exhibit apathy and short attention spans. Mindfulness training, along with an engaging and caring learning environment, can help students overcome their more complacent or anxious tendencies. This, in turn, helps students engage in the learning process, as attention is, of course, required for learning. If a student's brain drifts off task during a lesson on fractions, for example, it may be very hard for that student to fill in the gaps of the critical content. Teaching students mindfulness provides them with the tools to self-regulate and focus their attention for longer periods of time.

Next, we will discuss: (1) meditation and other mindfulness strategies and (2) unplugging.

## Meditation and Other Mindfulness Strategies

Contrary to what some people believe, meditation can be a secular practice that takes up very little time; it can be used effectively in as little as five minutes. Benefits include decreased anxiety, less vulnerability to pain, decreased tendencies toward depression and anger, and improved attention and empathy (Haidt, 2006; Ricard, 2010). With regular practice, meditation can also lead to self-acceptance, clear thinking, self-awareness, increased gray matter in parts of the brain that relate to attention and compassion, and other benefits. Meditation allows practitioners to get out of their own way in a sense by soothing their overstimulated, overstressed analytical minds and allowing them to direct their attention more effectively.

With consistent practice, practitioners of meditation increase their ability to concentrate for longer periods of time (Lutz, Slagter, Dunne, & Davidson, 2008). Meditation even influences brain waves—the electrical signals that indicate brain function and communication between neurons. Alpha waves occur when one is relaxed but alert and attentive, which is an ideal state for listening to teacher instruction. The results of a study researchers conducted at Brown University suggested that, over time, meditation may strengthen practitioners' brain responsiveness and ability to focus their attention for longer periods of time (Kerr et al., 2011). Meditation also triggers the parasympathetic nervous system, a part of the involuntary nervous system, which relaxes bodily functions such as heart rate and blood pressure. The effects of parasympathetic nervous system activation may also help students feel at peace, ease feelings of anxiety, and allow for clearer, more focused thinking (Hanson, 2009). Please consider the following six activities: (1) mindfulness meditation, (2) Why Meditate?, (3) body scans, (4) Eating a Raisin, (5) mindful listening, and (6) mindful walking.

## Mindfulness Meditation

Mindfulness meditation is a powerful and impactful activity. Ideally, teachers should utilize mindfulness meditation on a daily basis. In elementary schools, it is an ideal way to begin the day and an effective refocusing strategy following recess. Middle and high school teachers can use it for five minutes to begin class or for longer intervals during a block schedule or study hall. It is important to keep in mind that not all students will appreciate or want to partake in meditation. For those students who are uncomfortable or unwilling, we suggest that they choose another quiet activity such as silent reading or journaling. Consider the following three elements of this activity: (1) preparation, (2) essential learnings, and (3) directions.

### *Preparation*

We recommend that teachers try to practice meditation a number of times themselves before leading students in this activity. Teachers should also explain meditation (including the essential learnings) to students the first time they practice it and provide reminders or cues before subsequent sessions. With early elementary school students and students who are new to meditation, teachers should plan for short sessions, perhaps as short as two minutes. As students become more adept at meditation, teachers can utilize sessions as long as ten minutes. Teachers can use a timer or clock to keep track of the length of the session. A bell or chime can also be useful for signaling the start and end of the session.

### *Essential Learnings*

Teachers should help students understand the following information before asking them to engage in meditation.

- Meditation can be surprisingly difficult. The process itself is simple, but it is not easy to do successfully. It requires lots of practice, and people often have a hard time with it at first.

- It's okay to start with short meditations at first—even five minutes or less is both challenging and beneficial.

- If thoughts interrupt one's meditation and focus on breathing, notice the thoughts but let them go and return the focus to breathing.

- Deep breathing is from the diaphragm (muscles in the torso that expand and contract the lungs). The inhale should cause the abdomen or stomach area to expand. The exhale should cause the abdomen to contract. The chest moves very little during this type of breathing.

- Meditation has the most benefits when one practices it consistently over time.

### Directions

Teachers can use the following eight steps to guide mindfulness meditation in their classrooms.

1.  Ask students to sit cross-legged on the floor or upright in their chairs. They should find the middle ground between being comfortable and being rigid.

2.  Use a chime or bell to begin the session. Encourage students to listen to the sound until they can no longer hear it.

3.  Ask students to close their eyes and take several deep breaths in and out.

4.  Encourage them to relax their face and shoulders.

5.  Have them breathe out slowly, and breathe in slowly. Repeat this for ten cycles. For younger students, this can be modified to a lower number so they do not lose count.

6.  Describe how they can watch thoughts come and go, like popping a bubble. Encourage them to neither cling to their thoughts nor resist them. Suggesting that they imagine thoughts as clouds floating across the sky may help them with this.

7.  Continue this ten-breath cycle for five minutes at first (one to two minutes for young students) or longer with more experienced meditators.

8.  Ring the chime again to signal the end of the session. Encourage students to listen to the closing chime for as long as they can hear it. Then prompt them to rejoin the classroom when they are ready.

## Why Meditate?

Meditation is a skill that requires a disciplined practice to reap the most benefits. Why Meditate? is a simple activity that guides students in conceptualizing their reasons for meditating and can aid students in developing a disciplined practice (Kabat-Zinn, 1994). Since meditation's benefits are not always readily apparent, it is important for students to understand their own personal motives. A week or two after teaching students how to meditate, teachers could use Why Meditate? to introduce the many benefits of a consistent meditation practice. This activity is appropriate for all ages and could also be adapted to focus on mindfulness as a whole. Consider the following three elements: (1) preparation, (2) essential learnings, and (3) directions.

### Preparation

Each instance of Why Meditate? takes fifteen to twenty minutes. Teachers may wish to implement this activity multiple times with several weeks in between each iteration to gauge the effects of meditation practice. Students will need paper (perhaps in the form of a journal, which is useful for tracking responses over time) and writing utensils to complete this activity.

### Essential Learnings

The following points can help students understand why meditation is beneficial and begin to define their own reasons for meditating.

*   People can meditate for many reasons. These reasons include relaxation, improved emotional control, improved ability to focus, giving oneself time alone, and so on.

- Meditating regularly can be difficult because at times it may seem tedious or the benefits may not be readily apparent.

- Contemplating the *why* helps people stay more disciplined in their meditation practice.

### Directions

This discussion activity involves the following eight steps.

1. Have a discussion about the purposes and benefits of meditation.

2. Share the essential learnings of this lesson on meditation.

3. Ask students to jot down a list of reasons why they meditate or identify benefits of meditation they would like to experience.

4. Ask them to think about their values, the people they love, and their goals in life. Ask students to consider if they are paying attention to what they truly value in life.

5. Ask them to add their considerations to their list of reasons.

6. If students feel comfortable, encourage them to share ideas aloud.

7. As students hear ideas they like, invite them to capture those ideas in their journal.

8. Be sure to share your own reasons for being a practitioner of meditation.

## Body Scans

Body scans are a powerful mindfulness tool for students of all ages. Practicing mindful awareness of one's body enhances the ability to notice both physical sensations and mental events. The body scan activity decreases reactivity to stressors and increases one's ability to observe the passing of the various thoughts and feelings in which the mind generally engages (Carmody & Baer, 2008). Consider the following three elements: (1) preparation, (2) essential learnings, and (3) directions.

### Preparation

This activity is very easy to prepare for: it requires no materials, although teachers will want to plan how they will lead students through the body scan. It typically takes about ten minutes to complete this activity.

### Essential Learnings

Students should understand the following key aspects of a body scan.

- Taking time to be aware of the body allows people to notice stressed or tense muscles and relax them.

- Body scans help practice general focus and awareness, which can be applied to sensations in the body, thoughts in the mind, or external events.

- After learning body scan techniques, students can use them at any time.

### Directions

Body scans can be conducted in any order. The following eleven steps progress from the feet up to the head.

1. Ask students to lie comfortably on the floor or to sit up straight in their chairs. If seated, students should aim for the middle ground between being rigid and being relaxed. Ask them to rest their palms gently on the floor beside them or on their laps face up.

2. Invite students to take three to four slow belly breaths in and out.

3. Ask them to bring attention to their right foot. Have them notice the toes, the arch, and the heel touching the floor. Ask them to gently bring that awareness up to the calf and the thigh. Have them notice the feeling of the calf. Have them notice the pressure of the thigh against the floor or chair. Repeat with the left foot and leg.

4. Remind them to breathe in and out, slowly and gently, allowing their abdomen to rise and fall. Ask them to notice their torso, feeling their back against the carpet or chair, feeling the gentle rise and fall of their stomach.

5. Bring their attention to their ribcage. Ask them to feel their lungs expand and contract with each breath, in and out, in and out.

6. Invite them to notice the heart and how it beats on its own, without any conscious effort.

7. Invite them to move their attention to their right fingers and palms, their wrists, their arms, elbows, and shoulders. Repeat with the left arm.

8. Ask students to bring their awareness to their neck muscles. Invite them to relax their neck muscles. Ask them to notice their jaw muscles. Are they tight? Can they relax?

9. Invite them to notice their mouths, noses, eyes, and foreheads and relax the muscles of the face.

10. Ask them to notice their bodies as a whole. Invite them to outline their bodies in their minds starting at the crown of their head and imagining the outline traveling the course of the arm, down the right side, all the way around and up the left side, and resting again at the crown of the head.

11. Ask them to breathe deeply a few times. When they are ready, ask them to rejoin the class and calmly return to their seats.

## Eating a Raisin

Eating a Raisin (Spiegler & Guevremont, 2010) explores attention through taste and mindful eating. This activity is unlike anything most students have ever tried before—eating slowly and deliberately to experience every flavor and texture of the food. Eating a Raisin involves "relearning how to bring awareness to everyday activities so that you can see life as it is, unfolding moment by moment" (Williams & Penman, 2011, p. 78). Eating mindfully means using all of the senses and can bring an awareness of one's thoughts and feelings. It helps practitioners slow down and focus on the present moment. Further, it can help regulate eating habits by teaching practitioners to be aware of the food nourishing their bodies. Teachers can use this activity with students in grades K–12.

### *Preparation*

To conduct this ten-minute activity, each student needs to have one raisin. We suggest explaining the activity to students before passing out the raisins to ensure that they do not eat them before the activity has begun. Teachers should also be sure to accommodate any students with food allergies or dietary restrictions, and should substitute an acceptable and appropriate kind of food.

### *Essential Learnings*

Teachers can help students appreciate the purpose of Eating a Raisin through the following information.

- People often do things without paying much attention to them.

- Doing familiar activities slowly and deliberately allows one to see them from a new perspective.

- Many areas of life can benefit from the focus and attention practiced in this activity.

### *Directions*

The five steps of Eating a Raisin typically proceed as follows.

1. Students should hold the raisin in their hand and just look at it, as if they are seeing a raisin for the first time. Ask them to pretend they are a one-year-old, looking at and wondering what this wrinkled little item is all about. If their minds wander while doing this activity, ask students to gently return their attention to the activity.

2. Ask them to feel the raisin and rub it between their fingers. If students feel comfortable, ask them to close their eyes to limit the sensation to only that of touch.

3. Then ask them to place the raisin in their mouth without chewing it. Ask them to notice how it feels. Again, if they are comfortable, ask them to close their eyes for the experience.

4. Ask students to slowly chew their raisins. What does it taste like? Smell like? Feel like? Ask them not to rush into swallowing it. Finally, ask them to swallow it.

5. Lead the class in a discussion of what it's like not to rush through experiences. Where else might they be able to slow down and experience events with such attention?

## Mindful Listening

Mindful listening is a brief recurring activity that uses sounds as cues to inject moments of mindfulness throughout the day. One's environment is frequently filled with sounds and noises that go unnoticed. However, if people use sounds as cues to be more aware, they can practice being attentive to their environment and what they are doing in the moment. Noises from the environment give people the opportunity to practice mindful attentiveness—a skill that can help them develop an ability to direct their focus in a variety of situations. Consider the following three elements: (1) preparation, (2) essential learnings, and (3) directions.

### *Preparation*

Because teachers should use this activity spontaneously throughout the day, they should introduce and explain the process to students before implementing it for the first time.

### Essential Learnings

The following information explains the purposes behind this activity.

- Any sound can be a cue to be mindful.

- Mindful listening improves one's ability to focus and self-regulate.

- Listening is a skill that one can develop and practice.

### Directions

Mindful listening involves the following five steps.

1. Take the opportunity to incorporate this lesson when an unexpected sound occurs, such as a honking horn from outside or the sound of a bird.

2. Very softly, whisper "Listen." Pause for a moment before you speak again.

3. Quietly share with students the essential learnings.

4. Ask students to share ideas about when they can incorporate mindful listening into their school and home lives.

5. Ask students to share thoughts about interrupting and why people interrupt others during conversations.

## Mindful Walking

Mindful walking is an activity that raises students' awareness of their personal space and that of others' personal space. In a school setting, this can be beneficial in learning to set boundaries and respect others' physical space. By bringing conscious attention to what students often do unconsciously, teachers can help them practice mindful awareness. The goal of this activity is simply to be mindful of how and where one walks. Like sitting meditation, being mindful of how one walks can relieve stress, teach self-control, and induce a state of relaxation. Consider the following three elements: (1) preparation, (2) essential learnings, and (3) directions.

### Preparation

Mindful walking takes very little time to do and requires no materials. In addition to using this activity in a defined manner with the whole class, teachers can also remind students to walk mindfully at any time in the classroom, in the hallway or other areas of the school, and at recess.

### Essential Learnings

Students should understand and consider the following ideas as part of mindful walking.

- People have control over their bodies.

- People have full control of their movement and actions.

- Students can honor others' personal space by walking mindfully, with intention, and by noticing what they are doing.

***Directions***

A session of mindful walking typically uses the following eight-step process.

1.  Calmly ask or gesture to students to rise from their seats.

2.  Ask them to begin walking around the room and to be conscious of every step.

3.  Remind them to notice what they are doing with each step.

4.  Provide cue words such as to walk *calmly, carefully, gently,* and *thoughtfully.*

5.  Ask them to watch each step they take.

6.  Ask them to pause, take only one step, and freeze. Repeat this several times.

7.  You may want to include phrases such as, "You are leaving footprints of kindness wherever you go," "We want to be respectful and mindful of other people's space," and "Be mindful; be gentle."

8.  Ask students to gently, mindfully return to their seats. Ask them to mindfully pull out their chairs and be seated.

# Unplugging

While technology in and of itself is neither good nor bad, constant use of technology can be detrimental to one's ability to focus. With their constant feedback, devices frequently interrupt attempts at sustained attention (Christakis, 2011). Despite popular opinion, the brain cannot conduct two cognitive processes at the same time—it can only focus on one task at a time (Monk, Trafton, & Boehm-Davis, 2008; Sousa, 2011). What seems like multitasking is really task switching. According to Mark Bauerlein (2011), because students are able to task-switch so capably, they may not be developing the mental strength for cognitively complex tasks. When students constantly flit back and forth between learning and technological interruptions, it is difficult to achieve the depth of thinking required for challenging assignments. These interruptions also limit students' opportunities to practice remaining focused for extended periods of time. Note the following two strategies that can facilitate unplugging: (1) mindfully limiting technology at school and (2) mindfully limiting technology at home.

## Mindfully Limiting Technology at School

Technology does have a place in classrooms. Educators are having great success in using technology to improve students' engagement in learning. However, Bauerlein (2011) noted that task-switching and technology can prevent students from adequately learning to read and comprehend complex texts. He encouraged teachers to have classrooms where learning is unplugged for at least one hour per school day, during which students practice attending to complex, printed texts. As part of mindfulness instruction, teachers should encourage students to go for periods of time without checking their devices. To engage students in the importance of disconnecting from devices from time to time, teachers can lead students in a discussion of how to mindfully limit technology and what benefits this strategy might have. At the end of discussions, teachers and students can develop specific goals or classroom practices to limit technology use. For example, the class could decide to place their cell phones in a basket at the front of the classroom as they enter. If they are needed for class activities, students could then retrieve them. Consider the following three elements: (1) preparation, (2) essential learnings, and (3) directions.

### Preparation

This discussion and goal-setting activity can be modified for different age groups—younger students might have a fairly brief discussion, while older students may spend more time discussing the issue. Teachers can also plan to follow up with students after several days or a week to see how students feel about the goal after implementing it.

### Essential Learnings

Because some students may be resistant to reducing their technology use, teachers should share facts such as the following with students to provide reasons for limiting technology in class.

- Because the brain processes sequentially, it cannot multitask.

- Our brain can task-switch, or go back and forth between two tasks, which wastes precious neural energy and time.

- Task-switching slows productivity and increases errors.

### Directions

We recommend using the following five steps for this activity.

1. Share the essential learnings with students. Invite them to share their thoughts relevant to the topic.

2. Lead a discussion about how students can set mindful limits in their use of technology at school. Perhaps the classroom can be a technology-free zone for various times throughout the day.

3. Invite students to set a class goal for limiting technology in school. One example might be, "We will agree to give our mindful attention to learning for the first twenty minutes of class each day."

4. At a later date, ask them to discuss how successful they were with their goal and how they feel about their attempts.

5. Lead a discussion about stretching the goal.

## Mindfully Limiting Technology at Home

It is also important to help students understand the need for technology-free time at home. Turning off devices and televisions for even an hour a day can aid students in realizing how task-switching limits their focus. This activity also encourages students to communicate information about unplugging to parents. Consider the following three elements: (1) preparation, (2) essential learnings, and (3) directions.

### Preparation

Teachers should plan to hold an initial discussion to help students understand the benefits of limiting technology use at home and set goals as well as a follow-up discussion that allows students to share and reflect on their experiences.

### *Essential Learnings*

Helping students understand the following points will garner more support and appreciation for the idea of unplugging outside of school.

- Technology can limit one's ability to focus because it encourages task-switching.

- Task-switching slows productivity and increases errors.

- Unplugging benefits people socially, giving them more time to be present with others.

- Socializing with family and friends in face-to-face conversations builds emotional fluency and skills that are needed in day-to-day living as well as in the workforce.

### *Directions*

Discussion and goal setting around limiting technology use at home might follow these seven steps.

1. Share the essential learnings with students. Invite them to share their thoughts about each of the essential learnings.

2. Discuss times when students can mindfully limit the use of technology at home. For example, this may include setting aside technology during mealtimes. Ask them to consider how this might change the family dynamics and whether or not it would improve communication.

3. Challenge students to turn off all electronic devices including their cell phone, computer, television, radio, MP3 player, gaming consoles, and so on, for a set amount of time that stretches them slightly beyond their comfort zone.

4. Encourage them to write down their technology-use goal and the reasons behind the goal.

5. Ask them to consider what obstacles they might encounter. What strategies can they implement to overcome these obstacles?

6. Ask students to record what they observe and how they feel when they disconnect from their devices.

7. Upon returning to school, lead a discussion of how the process went.

## Summary

Attention is indeed a skill that educators can teach and students should practice. This chapter reviewed the importance of attention and detailed a number of activities for educators to use in the classroom and for students to try at home. From meditation to mindful eating to mindful walking, students (and teachers) have many tools at their disposal to engage in mindful attentiveness. Further, students can learn to use mindfulness tools to help them be less reactive and more proactive. In the next chapter, we describe how mindfulness practice can help develop and strengthen emotional control and outline relevant strategies that can be used in the classroom.

# Chapter 3: Comprehension Questions

1. How does mindfulness practice improve attention?

2. Why is practicing mindful attention important for students?

3. How does the Eating a Raisin activity help students practice attention?

4. Why can technology be detrimental to attention?

# Chapter 4

# EMOTIONAL CONTROL

Another intent of mindfulness practice is emotional control. This does not mean stifling emotions such as anxiety, sadness, or anger. Those types of feelings are normal and can often serve in useful ways. Emotions themselves are neither good nor bad, but it is important to develop strategies for managing negative or overwhelming emotions in a healthy, beneficial manner. Practicing mindfulness activities that enhance emotional control helps individuals learn to notice their emotions before responding, which reduces reactivity.

One can practice mindfulness both formally and informally as a method to bring awareness to emotions. Formally, practicing mindfulness on a regular basis has been shown to help practitioners control their responses, self-regulate, and strengthen their emotional control. Informally, simply learning to recognize negative emotions before reacting to a situation allows for a more thoughtful response.

Goleman (1998) described people with the emotional competence of self-control as those who "manage their impulsive feelings and distressing emotions well," "stay composed, positive, and unflappable even in trying moments," and "think clearly and stay focused under pressure" (p. 82). When people slow down to understand their emotions, they allow themselves the opportunity to choose how to respond and develop their ability to control how they react to the conflicts present in everyday life.

## Processes for Reacting Rationally

One of the simplest and most effective ways to help students react rationally to emotional situations is to directly teach processes for doing so. The following sections detail two activities along these lines: (1) awareness, analysis, and choice, and (2) the power to choose.

### Awareness, Analysis, and Choice

Awareness, analysis, and choice encourage students to pause and think about their actions and possible outcomes before they react. Fundamentally, the process outlined in this section asks students to consider their interpretations of situations and how these interpretations fuel their judgments and responses. Students then decide how they can adjust their reactions to achieve the most desirable outcome. When students develop an awareness of how interpretations affect instinctual responses, they become better equipped to consider many possible actions before reacting.

In *Managing the Inner World of Teaching*, Robert Marzano and Jana Marzano (2015) described emotional control as a three-phase process: (1) awareness, (2) analysis, and (3) choice. Table 4.1 shows the three phases and their related questions.

**Table 4.1: The Three Phases and Their Related Questions**

| Phase | Related Questions |
|---|---|
| Awareness | What emotions am I experiencing right now?<br>What is my interpretation of this situation? |
| Analysis | What actions will I probably execute as a result of my interpretation?<br>What will be the most probable outcome of my actions?<br>Will this outcome be the most positive for all concerned? |
| Choice | What is my preferred outcome?<br>What actions do I have to execute to attain this outcome? |

*Source: Adapted from Marzano & Marzano, 2015, p. 10.*

These three phases can serve as useful guides for both teachers and students. For example, if a teacher notices students passing notes in the back of the classroom, she could quickly bring her awareness to her own emotions by pausing and taking a moment to consider how she is interpreting the situation. Perhaps she finds herself assuming that the note is making fun of another student. She may feel angry or tense. By stopping to consider her usual behaviors in this situation, she can determine whether they are the best actions to take. Typically, she would stop class to confront the two students, which would shift the rest of the class's attention to the misbehaving students. By pausing in the analysis phase, even briefly, the teacher can determine a more positive course of action. She makes a conscious choice to get the class started in a think-pair-share activity while she calmly addresses the situation. She knows this will not embarrass those students and is a gentle way to set them back on task. Teachers who understand, label, and regulate their own emotions can manage their emotions more effectively and serve as healthy models for their students.

Teaching the three phases of awareness, analysis, and choice to students can help them use these processes in their own lives. For example, assume that one student bumps into another in the hallway. Depending on the student, his immediate reaction will vary. If he is prone to anger, he may react by punching the student who bumped into him. This could lead to a full-blown fight and disciplinary action for at least one of the students. However, if the student stops to analyze the situation, even briefly, he is likely to make a more thoughtful choice. He may realize, as he develops an awareness of his emotions, how quickly he tends to jump to anger. Then, by pausing to analyze the best course of action, he may give the student the benefit of the doubt and assume it was accidental. His choice, at least for now, is to ignore the fact that another student bumped into him. This is a much better outcome than if he had reacted without considering his response. Again, mindfulness widens the space between the stimulus (being bumped) and the response. Once teachers have instructed students about the three phases, they can lead students in a discussion of when students can use these techniques and why they might be useful. Consider the following three elements: (1) preparation, (2) essential learnings, and (3) directions.

## *Preparation*

Teachers will want to set aside time to instruct students on the awareness, analysis, and choice phases. For elementary school students, the explanation and discussion process may take twenty to thirty minutes; in middle and high school classrooms, more time may need to be set aside to accommodate longer discussions. Students will need writing utensils and paper to record their thoughts and reactions.

## *Essential Learnings*

Students should comprehend the following information about the awareness, analysis, and choice process.

- One can use mindfulness as a tool to regulate emotions and reactions.

- Reacting impulsively to a situation can lead to unintended, or even negative, consequences.

- Before reacting to a situation, a person can pause and run through a three-step thought process that includes awareness, analysis, and choice.

- *Awareness* means to consider the emotions one is experiencing and the assumptions or interpretations that are influencing those emotions.

- *Analysis* means to think about what actions one would likely take in a specific scenario, the outcome of these actions, and if there is a more preferable outcome.

- *Choice* means to take steps toward a preferred outcome by regulating the actions one executes.

## *Directions*

This discussion activity might involve the following six steps.

1. Explain the essential learnings and instruct students on the use of the three phases: awareness, analysis, and choice.

2. Describe an example scenario in which you used this process to make a decision, and list the questions you asked yourself in this situation.

3. Describe a scenario students might find themselves in. Ask them how they would instinctually react.

4. Have students list the questions they would ask themselves if they wanted to react mindfully using awareness, analysis, and choice.

5. After students consider the three phases of emotional control, ask them to describe what outcome they decided would be the most desirable. How would they achieve this outcome?

6. Have students identify other scenarios, either ones they have experienced in real life or ones they could reasonably imagine themselves experiencing, and explain how they could use the three-step process to regulate their emotions and reactions.

## The Power to Choose

The power to choose is another activity that helps students realize that they have a choice in their responses to stimuli. It involves teaching students about choosing their reactions and helping them plan for emotional events in the future. Consider the following three elements: (1) preparation, (2) essential learnings, and (3) directions.

### Preparation

This discussion activity requires little preparation or materials. It is often helpful, however, to provide students with a visual representation of the relationships between stimulus, choice, and response, either by drawing it on the board or creating a handout.

### Essential Learnings

The following points can be useful in instruction and discussion for this activity.

- Proactive people focus on things they can control and choose the best response to a situation before reacting.

- Reactive people respond emotionally without thinking. They also fixate on things they can't control and blame external factors when things go wrong.

- A stimulus is a situation or event that causes a person to think, feel, or act a certain way. How a person reacts to a stimulus is called a response.

### Directions

When instructing students about thoughtful responses, teachers might use the following five steps.

1. Explain the meaning of stimulus and response by drawing two connecting squares on the board labeled *Stimulus* and *Response* (see figure 4.1). Explain that when it comes to emotional reactions, the stimulus is the external event that prompts an emotion, and the response is how the person reacts. If stimulus and response are directly connected to each other, the person will react immediately based on the first emotion he or she feels. Give an example of a stimulus and how one might instinctually respond.

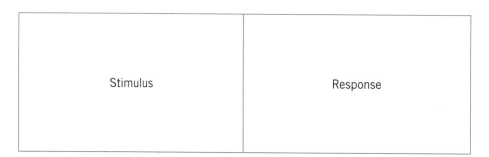

**Figure 4.1: Stimulus and automatic or instinctual response.**

2. Explain that with mindfulness, the goal is to put a gap between stimulus and response. Draw two new squares on the board (again labeled *Stimulus* and *Response*) with a gap or space between them. Write the word *Choice* between the squares (see figure 4.2). Explain that the space represents taking a moment to pause and determine the best response to a situation, which allows a person to be proactive instead of reactive. Invite students to discuss the difference between proactive and reactive.

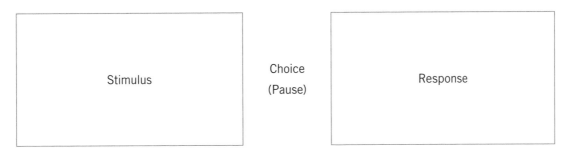

**Figure 4.2: Stimulus, choice, and response.**

3.  There are a number of strategies that can help a person pause before reacting. Encourage students to brainstorm some ideas with you. Ideas may include counting to ten, taking a deep belly breath, waiting until you cool down or feel calm, and so on.

4.  Write the following prompt on the board: "When I feel angry, frustrated, or upset, I will . . ." Invite students to develop their own lists.

5.  Encourage students to share ideas from their lists. Then ask students why they think mindfulness training helps widen the space between stimulus and response.

## Strategies for Managing Overwhelming and Negative Emotions

In order to help students control their emotions, educators can teach strategies to that end and have students practice these strategies in the classroom. The following sections detail three activities to help students develop greater emotional control: (1) watching one's thoughts, (2) internalizing the positive, and (3) naming and taming one's emotions.

### Watching One's Thoughts

Part of emotional control involves being aware of but not consumed by one's moods: "When unhappiness or stress hovers overhead, rather than taking it all personally, you learn to treat them as if they were black clouds in the sky, and to observe them with friendly curiosity as they drift past" (Williams & Penman, 2011, p. 5). In essence, mindfulness allows practitioners to catch negative thought patterns before they become all-consuming. Mindfulness is not about changing all of one's negative thoughts to positive ones. Rather, it encourages observing the thoughts without getting ensnared by them.

Watching one's thoughts involves teaching students a simple four-step process for disconnecting from negative emotions (Divine, 2014): (1) notice the negative thought or feeling, (2) use a power statement to interrupt negativity, (3) replace negativity with positive self-talk and visualization, and (4) reinforce the positive mental state with a power statement or pose. Teaching students that the thoughts that float through their minds are not the thoughts they necessarily need to entertain can help them better manage their feelings, such as those of self-doubt or anxiety. Consider the following three elements: (1) preparation, (2) essential learnings, and (3) directions.

#### *Preparation*

Teachers can prepare for this fifteen- to thirty-minute activity by coming up with example power statements, power poses, and situations in which students might use this process. It's important to discuss with students the idea that everyone has negative thoughts that come and go throughout the day. It's where a person puts his or her focus that matters.

### Essential Learnings

In addition to the process for replacing negative thinking, students can be made aware of the following information so that they understand the purpose of this activity.

- Mindfulness is not about pretending people don't have negative thoughts. However, mindfulness is about witnessing and letting go of one's negative thoughts.

- Not all thoughts are worthy of one's attention and energy.

- People have the power to catch their negative feelings and interrupt them before they are overwhelmed by them.

- Replacing negative thinking with empowering thoughts helps people be successful in stressful situations. This technique is even used by U.S. Navy SEALs (Divine, 2014).

### Directions

The following four steps outline the discussions associated with this activity.

1. Invite students to think of times when they are vulnerable to negative thinking. This may be when they are tired, uncomfortable, in a new situation, or feeling alone. Pose the following discussion question or a similar one: Instead of allowing negativity to catch you off guard in these situations, what might noticing negativity look like, sound like, and feel like?

2. Once negative thinking has been noticed, it can be stopped through the use of power statements. Some power statements include phrases such as "I can do this," "I am powerful," and "I love a challenge." Ask students to form pairs or small groups and create three or more of their own power statements to share with the class.

3. Ask students to imagine how they would like events to play out in a difficult situation. For example, instead of sitting alone in the lunchroom, what might it look like, sound like, and feel like to comfortably sit with friends? Or, what might it look like to work hard to prepare for an upcoming test and then succeed by earning a high score?

4. Suggest that students adopt a power slogan coupled with a power move to help themselves overcome negative thoughts. For example, "I got this!" is a strong phrase or mantra that captures a "bring it on" attitude. Students could match this phrase with an empowering move such as holding their arms up high in a victory pose. Encourage students to try out different phrases and stances and to share their power phrases and power moves.

## Internalizing the Positive

People can learn optimism. One way to think about optimism is through the lens of explanatory styles—the ways in which people choose to view or explain what occurs in their lives. Martin Seligman (2006) described three dimensions of explanatory style, as follows.

1. **Permanence:** Are events temporary or permanent?

2. **Pervasiveness:** Do events affect one's whole life or stay compartmentalized?

3. **Personalization:** Are events internally or externally controlled?

Table 4.2 depicts how optimists and pessimists use these three aspects of explanatory style to color their perception of both good and bad events.

**Table 4.2: Three Dimensions of Explanatory Style**

| Dimension | Event Type | Optimistic | Pessimistic |
|---|---|---|---|
| Permanence | Bad things | **Temporary:** Temporary circumstances in my life cause the bad things that happen to me. | **Permanent:** Permanent elements of my life cause the bad things that happen to me. |
| | Good things | **Permanent:** Permanent elements of my life cause the good things that happen to me. | **Temporary:** Temporary circumstances in my life cause the good things that happen to me. |
| Pervasiveness | Bad things | **Specific:** When a bad thing happens in one area of my life, it doesn't negatively affect other parts of my life. | **Universal:** When a bad thing happens in one area of my life, it ruins my whole life. |
| | Good things | **Universal:** When a good thing happens in one area of my life, it makes my whole life better. | **Specific:** When a good thing happens in one area of my life, it doesn't positively affect other parts of my life. |
| Personalization | Bad things | **External:** A bad thing happened to me because of factors out of my control. | **Internal:** A bad thing happened to me because I didn't do something right. |
| | Good things | **Internal:** A good thing happened to me because I did something right. | **External:** A good thing happened to me because of factors out of my control. |

*Source: Marzano & Marzano, 2015, p. 70.*

This activity (Hanson, 2009) helps students focus on the positive aspects of life and develop a positive outlook. Consider the following three elements: (1) preparation, (2) essential learnings, and (3) directions.

### Preparation

This activity requires some direct instruction on learning an optimistic outlook, which teachers should prepare in advance. Students should also have paper and writing utensils for the journaling portion of the activity.

### Essential Learnings

The following points can be useful as teachers explain the importance of optimism and how to seek out optimism in daily life.

- It is natural for people to pay more attention to negative events, due to how the brain processes these events.

- However, people can learn to focus on positive experiences, thus training their brains to actively notice the good things in life.

- Many positive things often go unnoticed, such as a beautiful sunrise, stars in the sky, a leaf falling from a tree, a smile from a friend, or the taste of a crisp apple.

- Optimism also involves curbing the negative things one says to oneself, even when experiencing a difficult or discouraging event.

### *Directions*

Internalizing the positive is conducted through the following five steps.

1. Share with students the essential learnings. Ask them to describe positive things that often go unnoticed.

2. Take a brief walk (preferably outdoors) during which students must actively seek out positive things. Ask them to mentally and quietly note the positive things.

3. Encourage them, using a calm voice, to try to expand their positive feelings. Encourage them to try to experience the positive feelings throughout their bodies.

4. Upon returning to the classroom, ask students to journal about the experience.

5. Elicit willing students to share their thoughts.

## Naming and Taming One's Emotions

People have the innate tendency to give more immediate attention to negative events and emotions such as anger, fear, guilt, and regret (Rozin & Royzman, 2001). When something negative occurs, people may feel as if their responses are beyond their control. However, widening the space between stimulus and response begins by reflecting on one's own emotional intelligence. Marc Brackett and Dena Simmons (2015) defined five skills of emotional intelligence: (1) recognizing emotions, (2) understanding emotions, (3) labeling emotions, (4) expressing emotions, and (5) regulating emotions. Teachers can ask themselves and students questions such as the following to gauge their levels of emotional intelligence.

- **Recognizing emotions:** "How often do I recognize emotions in myself and others?"

- **Understanding emotions:** "Can I identify triggers for specific emotions?"

- **Labeling emotions:** "Do I discuss and label emotions for my own understanding and for others' understanding?"

- **Expressing emotions:** "Am I comfortable expressing a wide range of emotions? Do I recognize cultural differences in expressing emotions?"

- **Regulating emotions:** "What strategies do I use to regulate my feelings? Which of these strategies are effective?"

Consider the following three elements: (1) preparation, (2) essential learnings, and (3) directions.

### *Preparation*

Students will need paper or journals and writing utensils for this activity.

### *Essential Learnings*

Teachers should convey the following information to students during this activity.

- Having an awareness of the subtleties of various feelings helps people more effectively control their emotions.

- Taming one's emotions does not mean that one stops feeling emotions. It does mean that a person does not act on his or her feelings without thoughtful consideration.

- When people have unpleasant or negative emotions, they can respond to them in a healthy manner that reduces these feelings' intensity:

    - When people are stressed, they can use deep breathing exercises.

    - When people are angry, they can count to ten several times.

- With practice, choosing more effective responses gets easier and easier.

### *Directions*

Using the following five steps, teachers can help students learn to identify and control their emotions.

1. Ask students to write about one or more strong emotions that they would label as unpleasant or negative that they've felt in the past week.

2. Ask them to describe the emotion as vividly as possible. For example, if a student describes how she felt after being left out of a game her friends were playing, she might say that she felt lonely, angry, or as though her friends didn't really care about her feelings. She could also describe physical sensations, such as a tightness in the pit of her stomach.

3. For each emotion they choose to write about, ask them to describe how they handled that emotion.

4. Have them consider whether they could improve the way they managed an emotion or situation.

5. Invite students to share if they feel comfortable. Suggest appropriate ways to handle strong emotions. For example, a teacher might suggest that students express their emotions by talking calmly to the person who is upsetting them or bring clarity to an upsetting situation by trying to understand why another person might act a certain way.

## Summary

Emotions are neither good nor bad, but strong negative emotions can sometimes dominate one's thoughts to the point that they affect how a person acts and feels for a significant period of time. Mindfulness helps practitioners develop an awareness of their emotions and strengthens their control over their responses. Mindfulness is not about avoiding or preventing negative feelings completely. Rather, it is about not letting negative thoughts control one's mood and outlook. This chapter discussed processes for reacting rationally to stressful situations and strong emotions. It also offered other tools to help students learn the art of emotional control, including watching one's thoughts, internalizing the positive, and naming and taming one's emotions. The next chapter provides additional mindfulness tools that can help students and teachers maintain a positive outlook and self-concept.

# Chapter 4: Comprehension Questions

1. What is emotional control?

2. Describe each phase of the awareness, analysis, and choice process.

3. Why is optimism important to emotional control?

# Chapter 5

# POSITIVE SELF-CONCEPT

*Self-concept* is the view people have of themselves and their abilities. A positive self-concept is a result of having both a strong sense of self-efficacy as well as high self-esteem. *Self-efficacy* means knowing one has the ability to achieve goals through dedication and hard work. *Self-esteem* is one's overall sense of self-worth. Self-concept, and particularly self-efficacy, has been shown to have a moderate to significant impact on students' achievement and goal attainment (Hattie, 2009). The increase in confidence that accompanies a positive self-concept also develops students' resiliency, as it helps them perceive themselves as capable of overcoming obstacles. Conversely, a negative self-concept can significantly impact students' motivation to set and work toward goals; their lack of confidence or low expectations may cause them to expect failure before they even try.

Teachers and parents can directly influence students' development and maintenance of a positive self-concept. One powerful method teachers can use to help students develop a positive self-concept is to model how a person with a positive self-concept approaches problems, tasks, and daily interactions. When teachers share with students how much they personally value self-acceptance, effort toward goals, and a willingness to take risks, they are influencing students to similarly value these qualities. Another method teachers can use to encourage a positive self-concept is providing specific feedback related to effort. For example, a teacher might say, "Your essay is well organized and has almost no grammatical mistakes—I can tell you really worked hard on this!" When teachers do this, students' self-efficacy and self-esteem improve. Further, encouraging and helping students experience positive emotions and challenge their negative thoughts about themselves also bolster students' self-concept.

This chapter introduces tools that teachers can implement in a relatively short amount of time to help students enhance their positive emotions and develop self-acceptance. Specifically, this chapter details three types of strategies: (1) strategies related to body language, (2) mood boosters, and (3) strategies related to self-compassion. The more students practice these and other self-concept strategies, the more natural they will become. Some tools may be a better fit than others for certain students. Encourage students to regularly utilize the ones that work for them and to continue noticing behaviors and attitudes that boost their self-concept and those that do not. With practice and time, students can retrain their brains to develop positive theories of self.

## Strategies Related to Body Language

Body language communicates messages to others, but it also influences how a person feels about him- or herself. For example, expansive, confident body language increases the body's level of testosterone, which can make a person feel more powerful (Cuddy, 2015). In one study, participants were asked to participate in powerful poses such as standing like a superhero and expanding one's body. Another group was asked to assume low-power poses such as slumping or minimizing one's apparent size. Participants were to hold the poses for two minutes. The results indicated that "the high-power posers showed a 19 percent increase in testosterone and a 25 percent decrease in cortisol. Low-power posers showed the opposite pattern—a 10 percent decrease in testosterone and a 17 percent increase in cortisol" (Cuddy, 2015, p. 205). Higher testosterone levels can increase feelings of confidence and strength, whereas cortisol rises in tandem with levels of anxiety and stress (Cuddy, 2015).

Teachers can instruct students on the power of body language by incorporating activities—such as Walking the Walk and power poses—that allow students to experience the dramatic influence posture and movement can have on one's level of confidence and state of being.

### Walking the Walk

This activity incorporates physical movement and asks students to examine how body language relates to confidence. It is appropriate for students in grades K–12.

#### Preparation

This activity takes between five and fifteen minutes, and no materials are needed.

#### Essential Learnings

The following information can help students understand the importance and influence of body language.

- People's physiology affects their moods or states of mind.

- Slight adjustments to people's physiology can improve their moods or states of mind.

- If done regularly, people can use strategies (such as the way they stand or walk) to improve their self-confidence.

#### Directions

Teachers can lead students through the following six body language experiences.

1. Invite students to think about public figures or celebrities who walk with confidence.

2. Ask students to walk around the classroom as if they were feeling unconfident—perhaps slouching or looking at the ground.

3. Then ask students to walk with confidence. Provide prompts such as "raise your head and focus your gaze in front of you" or "put your shoulders back and your chest forward."

4. Have them discuss the differences they felt with the slight adjustment in their physiology.

5. Share with them the essential learnings.

6. Ask them how adjusting their physiology could benefit them in certain areas of their life.

## Power Poses

Teachers can instruct students about power poses in five to ten minutes and then interweave them periodically throughout the school day to boost students' energy levels and confidence. This activity is appropriate for all ages.

### Preparation

Teachers may want to practice the poses ahead of time in order to most effectively model them for students.

### Essential Learnings

- The way we carry our body affects our moods.

- If we carry ourselves in an open, expansive pose, it increases levels of testosterone within the body, which gives you a feeling of confidence and strength (Cuddy, 2015).

- Poses that make the body look small, such as slouching, lead to increased levels of cortisol, which is related to stress (Cuddy, 2015), and make it harder to learn (Mayo Clinic, 2016).

- Just by adjusting our posture when we walk or sit, we can adjust our moods.

### Directions

This body language activity involves trying out four low- and high-power poses. Once students have tried all four poses, they should discuss the differences they felt in this comparison activity.

1. **Low-power pose:** Ask students to slump down in their desk or chair with eyes cast downward. Invite them to try saying "I'm having a great day" as if they mean it.

2. **High-power pose:** Ask students to stand up tall and proud, perhaps in a superhero pose. Have them say "I'm having a great day" as if they mean it.

3. **Walking low-power pose:** Ask students to try walking with shoulders slumped and their heads down, at a slow, dragging pace. Invite them to greet their classmates.

4. **Walking high-power pose:** Ask students to walk with their chests held high. Encourage them to look their classmates in the eyes, smile, and greet them.

## Mood Boosters

A person's moods will vary from day to day and even moment to moment. This is completely normal (Lyubomirsky, 2008; Pasricha, 2016), but there are times when people may want to improve their moods so they can be more productive, feel happier, be more focused, or do their best in school and at home. A student can adjust his or her mood to a more positive one in a short amount of time. Once learned, teachers can use the activities in the following sections in the classroom or any time a student (or teacher) wants to adjust their mood. We offer two proven mood boosters: (1) power-ups and (2) random acts of kindness.

### Power-Ups

Throughout the day, teachers may find that students benefit from a quick emotional or energy boost. *Power-ups* are accessible strategies students can utilize when they are feeling lethargic, moody, or despondent. Jane McGonigal described power-ups (2015) as things a person can do to lift his or her mood and might include activities such as exercising, listening to music, or talking to a friend. McGonigal developed the idea of power-ups while struggling with depression and debilitating physical symptoms due to an improperly healed concussion. Before this event, McGonigal had studied the psychology of video games, which she found improved users' optimism, determination, and mood. She realized, after over a month of disheartening bed rest, that she could combat her negative thoughts and desire to give up by treating her recovery like a video game. In a video game, power-ups give a character special powers or a special boost; for McGonigal, power-ups were activities that lifted her spirits and lessened her symptoms.

Teachers can apply the concept of power-ups in the classroom by helping students identify activities they can do when they have pessimistic thoughts, feel unmotivated, or want to give up. This strategy closely relates to emotional control and emotional intelligence as it challenges students to recognize when they need to activate a power-up to improve their mood. Developing and implementing power-ups can help students gain an awareness of their feelings and can help them understand that they ultimately have control over the permanence of their emotions. Consider the following three elements: (1) preparation, (2) essential learnings, and (3) directions.

### Preparation

Teachers can set aside fifteen to twenty minutes to discuss the concept of power-ups with students and to help them create their own lists of power-ups. Students will need journals or paper and writing utensils to record their lists. Teachers may also provide chart paper and markers so that students can record a collaborative list of power-ups to share with the classroom.

### Essential Learnings

Teachers can explain power-ups to students using the following points.

- In video games, power-ups give characters extra power or special boosts that can help them overcome a challenge.

- People can develop their own power-ups by doing activities that help them overcome obstacles or negative thinking in their lives. These activities are free and easy to use, and students can complete them in a short amount of time.

- Accumulating power-ups is when people come up with lists of boosts that help them feel better when they are discouraged or depressed.

- Activating power-ups is when people implement one of their power-ups.

- Some examples of power-ups include deep belly breaths, listening to a favorite song, humming for one full minute, and smiling (even when you don't feel like it).

### Directions

This activity typically involves the following five steps.

1. Discuss with students the essential learnings of power-ups—what they are, why someone would use them, and when one would use them.

2. Have students journal quietly for three to five minutes, encouraging them to come up with at least five ideas for power-ups that have worked or may work for them personally.

3. Divide students into groups of two or three. On large chart paper, have students list ten or more power-ups to share with the class.

4. Try out a few of the power-ups together.

5. Discuss with students how the power-ups affected their moods and any observations they made about the process.

## Random Acts of Kindness

Sonja Lyubomirsky, a professor of psychology at the University of California, Riverside, has posited that 10 percent of our happiness is based on circumstances outside of our control, while the other 90 percent is within our control (2008). Her research has shown that helping others—an activity very much within one's control—is energizing and leads to much higher levels of happiness and contentment. Students (and teachers) of any age can perform random acts of kindness. Here, we'll discuss three important elements to consider: (1) preparation, (2) essential learnings, and (3) directions.

### Preparation

The initial discussion can last anywhere from fifteen to thirty minutes. Students will need journals or paper to capture their thoughts, or the teacher can write students' ideas on a whiteboard or on chart paper. Students will have to engage in the actual acts of kindness on their own time, but teachers will want to schedule time for a follow-up discussion so students can share their experiences.

### Essential Learnings

Teachers can share the following key points with students about random acts of kindness.

- Kindness toward yourself and others is good for you (Lyubomirsky, 2008).

- Doing kind things for others can, in turn, make you happy. Some people have called this a *helper's high* (Pasricha, 2016).

- There are unlimited opportunities for random acts of kindness within your school, home, neighborhood, and community. You don't have to look far.

- Random acts of kindness bring greater happiness to you if you are not forced to do them. You need to perform these acts of kindness of your own free will (Lyubomirsky, 2008).

- Students should perform random acts of kindness out of generosity, without a desire for or expectation of thanks or rewards.

### Directions

A general process for this activity is outlined in these five steps.

1. Ask students if they've ever heard of random acts of kindness. Together, devise a definition of "random acts of kindness." For example, one definition might be, "Random acts of kindness are when you do nice things for someone else when they are not expecting it. They may not even know who did the act of kindness."

2. Prompt students to give examples they've seen on the news or witnessed at school, at home, in the community, and in the world. Point out that acts of kindness do not have

to be large to make a difference. Examples might include holding the door for someone, raking leaves for an elderly neighbor, or doing extra chores around the house without someone asking.

3.  Share the essential learnings with students. Have a discussion about them. Some discussion questions may include, "Why do you think being kind to others is good for you?" "Have you ever done a nice thing for someone, but the recipient never knew it was you who did it?" "How did that feel?" "Have you ever been forced to do something nice for someone?" "How did that compare to something you decided to do on your own?"

4.  Ask students to brainstorm in their journal or as a class random acts of kindness they'd be willing to try in their own lives.

5.  After a few days have passed, follow up and ask students to share their experiences with random acts of kindness. Encourage them to continue random acts of kindness by varying when and what they choose to do.

## Strategies Related to Self-Compassion

Students' self-concepts can have a tremendous influence on the expectations and descriptions they attribute to themselves (Hattie, 1992). It is often easy for students to focus on their failures or weaknesses, which in turn limits the goals and expectations they set for themselves. One way students can improve their self-concept is through the use of self-compassion. *Self-compassion*, as defined by Kristin Neff (2011), means to respond to one's own struggles and problems with consideration and empathy. Students who practice self-compassion should try not to rush to judgment when they reflect on themselves, their actions, or their achievements. Instead, students should treat themselves like they would treat a person they deeply care for; they should encourage themselves, advocate for their own success, and respond to failure optimistically.

Self-compassion relates to mindfulness in that it requires one to recognize negative perceptions about oneself without the usual judgments that may accompany these thoughts. Aspects of self-compassion, such as limiting judgment and understanding that everyone is imperfect, can also help reduce feelings of isolation and instances of anxiety, depression, and rumination (Neff, 2011). The following three activities—(1) being kind to ourselves, (2) participating in a self-compassion art activity, and (3) sending letters to our former selves—relate strategies students can use to develop self-compassion, and by extension, a more positive self-concept.

### Being Kind to Ourselves

Patterns of positive thinking can help people view themselves, situations, and others in beneficial, positive ways. Additionally, being kind to oneself and realizing that no one is perfect builds a positive self-concept and sense of self-efficacy. However, in order for students to manage challenges and negative thought patterns, they must have strategies they can use to support themselves and their success.

Replacing a negative self-image with a positive image often begins with changing the words one uses to refer to oneself. Being kind to ourselves is an activity that challenges students to use positive words and phrases to develop compassion for themselves. Because this activity can be an emotional one, it is best to use it after teachers have implemented many of the other mindfulness tools. This activity is appropriate for all ages, though it is best suited to small groups or classrooms with an established environment of trust.

### Preparation

This short, five-minute activity requires no materials. Teachers can use the prompts in the directions section to guide students through the activity.

### Essential Learnings

Explaining the following points to students before conducting this activity will help them understand the purpose behind it.

- Sometimes people are not kind to themselves. Sometimes people think or say mean things about themselves, such as "I'm stupid" or "I have no friends." This can lead to anxiety, stress, and poor health.

- With practice, one can learn to be kind toward himself or herself.

- Kindness toward oneself leads to kindness toward others.

- No one is perfect, and everyone faces challenges he or she must overcome.

### Directions

Teachers can guide students through this activity using the following six-step process.

1. Ask students to sit comfortably. If they feel comfortable doing so, have them close their eyes.

2. Ask them to think of someone or something they love. Instruct them to think about how they feel when interacting with this person or object. What things do they say or do to show their love?

3. Then ask them to think of someone who loves them. Have them think about how this person expresses his or her love and how they feel when they understand that person cares for them. What kind words or phrases does that person use to show he or she cares for them?

4. Now ask them to direct those feelings of love toward themselves. Encourage them to replace negative thoughts about themselves with positive self-talk, such as "I am lovable," or "I can succeed if I keep trying."

5. Ask students to return their focus to the classroom when they are ready.

6. The next tasks in the classroom should be quieter, allowing for a gentle transition back to learning.

## Participating in a Self-Compassion Art Activity

This activity allows students the opportunity to select self-affirming thoughts, improve self-concept, and express their creativity.

### Preparation

The time constraints and materials for this activity vary. Teachers could simply provide students with white paper and markers, crayons, or colored pencils, but they might also use colored construction paper, glue, and scissors; paint and brushes; or three-dimensional features such as feathers and foam pieces.

### Essential Learnings

Discuss the following information with students to lend specific purpose to this creative activity.

- Being kind to oneself is the beginning of mindfulness.

- When people are good to themselves, they have more to give others.

- Being kind to oneself builds self-acceptance and a positive self-concept.

### Directions

The four steps of this activity are as follows.

1. After a brief discussion of the importance of self-compassion and empathy toward oneself and others, brainstorm some affirmations that reflect those ideas. Examples of affirming statements that reflect self-compassion include "I am good enough," "I can overcome the problems I face," and "I have many strengths."

2. Invite students to choose one or more affirmations that resonate with them. Encourage students to vary them so there are many different messages to display in the classroom or around the school.

3. Ask students to create a poster or visual representation of one of the affirming statements.

4. As an optional step, invite students to present their posters or visual representations to the class. In the presentation, encourage students to describe why they chose a particular affirming statement and the significance of the colors, shapes, and textures they chose to use.

## Sending Letters to Our Former Selves

Sending letters to our former selves is a powerful reflection activity that encourages students to revisit how they were in the past and come to terms with their decisions, their values, and how they handled challenges. This activity can help students recognize how they have grown and changed as an individual and allow them to accept the imperfect aspects of their history. It also enables them to explicitly describe life lessons they have learned and can carry into the future. This activity is most appropriate for students who are able to reflect on their past experiences and write several paragraphs independently.

### Preparation

This activity will take approximately thirty minutes, and students will need writing utensils and paper or journals to record their thoughts.

### Essential Learnings

The following points can help students understand the purpose of this activity.

- As people mature, they gain wisdom.

- People who reflect on what they have learned are more apt to recognize how they have changed.

- Self-awareness can help people continue to grow and change.

- By expressing reflections in writing, people can more easily remember those lessons and insights for the future.

### Directions

This activity involves the following four steps.

1. Ask students to write letters to their former selves. This letter is from their wiser current selves.

2. Invite them to think about what they could say to their younger selves that would help them in the future.

3. Share a sample letter, such as the one in figure 5.1, to help students begin their drafts.

4. If students are comfortable, invite them to share passages or important lessons from their letters. Teachers can also discuss with students how this activity changed their perception of who they are and how they can approach conflicts and obstacles in the future.

---

Dear Jeanie's Eighteen-Year-Old Self,

Life awaits you, sweet girl! Pack lightly so you don't have a lot of baggage to carry around. This letter reminds you what to take with you as you journey forward into life, and, perhaps even more importantly, what to leave behind.

Remember to pack self-love. I'm not referring to egotistical love of self, but rather a tender, accepting, compassionate love. You're going to make mistakes; that's part of the journey. Remember not to be hard on yourself. Look for and honor your strengths. Grow your talents. Walk tall.

Once your self-love is packed for the journey, love of others comes quite naturally. Wherever you travel, look for what is right in others. Shine the light on their goodness. Forgive them, for at times, people will do you wrong. Love them anyway.

It's very important to take along courage. Events will happen in your life that will catch you off guard and knock you to your knees. You will lose people you love, and the pain will seem unbearable. Your heart will be broken at least one time. You may not get every job you apply for. Courage will help you move forward, even when you want to crawl under the covers and stay there. Courage will allow you to step up, again and again, when life is hard.

---

**Figure 5.1: Sample letter to former self.**

Continued on next page →

What to leave behind? One thing to definitely leave behind is comparing yourself to others. All of us are born with unique gifts to offer the world. The world would be a dull place without our distinct differences. So instead of comparing yourself, work on developing your unique gifts. Then your energy will be better spent.

Also, please do not plan on carrying the idea of trying to be perfect. Perfection is an impossible goal, and is not a healthy frame of mind. It is much better to be perfectly imperfect. Instead, focus on giving your best each day. This will give you peace of mind and better serve our world.

In closing, remember you are enough. You are loved. Always.

Love,

Your Future Self

## Summary

Teachers and the choices they make in the classroom can influence students' self-concept. It is important to keep in mind that building a positive self-concept is a process, not a destination. We discussed three important approaches: (1) strategies related to body language, (2) mood boosters, and (3) strategies related to self-compassion. This chapter described several activities that can help students improve their self-concepts: (1) Walking the Walk, (2) power poses, (3) power-ups, (4) random acts of kindness, (5) being kind to ourselves, (6) participating in a self-compassion art activity, and (7) sending letters to our former selves. Teachers can reinforce these specific tools, such as confident body language or compassionate self-talk, on a daily basis to help build students' confidence and esteem over time. The changes brought about by teaching students how to boost their self-concept are subtle but have the potential to make a significant difference in students' overall well-being, happiness, and achievement. The next chapter relates strategies that further enhance students' emotional mindfulness and can help them strengthen their interpersonal relationships.

# Chapter 5: Comprehension Questions

1. Define self-concept, self-efficacy, and self-esteem.

2. How does body language affect self-concept?

3. What is self-compassion?

# Chapter 6

# POSITIVE INTERACTIONS

Increased focus on mindfulness can enhance a student's ability to engage in positive interactions with others. Mindfulness helps students increase the think-time between stimulus and response, thus giving them the chance to slow down, consider others' thoughts and feelings, and consider their options before taking action. This allows students to respond less impulsively, thus improving the chances for positive interactions with peers, staff, and parents.

Encouraging positive interactions among students (and with other people in the learning environment) helps to build a school and classroom atmosphere that promote learning and improve school-wide culture (Bernard, 2004). Examples of positive interactions include listening, being compassionate, respecting others' personal space, encouraging and supporting others, expressing gratitude, and using manners. Nonexamples include behaviors such as criticizing, gossiping, hitting, bullying, blaming, interrupting, controlling, and not listening.

In one survey, teachers expressed that poor student behavior is the second biggest problem in school, just behind lack of interest (Bridgeland et al., 2013). For this reason, it is essential to provide students with tools to help strengthen their social-emotional skills, of which positive interactions are a central part. Students with positive peer interactions are more likely to have strong friendships and be more engaged in class. Further, if students' peers accept them, they are more likely to utilize prosocial behaviors in school. Students who do not experience positive interactions often exhibit negative behavior, which affects achievement and general well-being (Sebanc, 2003). Additionally, if students have positive interactions with their teachers, they are more likely to demonstrate confidence and academic success (Stuhlman & Pianta, 2009).

Positive peer and teacher-student interactions build a solid foundation for the classroom environment and improve the likelihood that students will continue to experience positive events related to school (Stuhlman & Pianta, 2009). Additionally, students can gain a sense of safety and belonging through positive interactions. When students feel accepted and safe in a particular environment, they are better able to focus on tasks that require advanced cognitive processes. Robert Marzano, Darrell Scott, Tina Boogren, and Ming Lee Newcomb (2017) used Maslow's hierarchy of needs (Maslow, 1943, 1969) to explain how safety and belonging are essential to creating an effective and inspirational classroom. In Maslow's model, (1) physiology, (2) safety, (3) belonging, (4) esteem within a community, (5) self-actualization, and (6) connection to something greater than self make up the six levels of a needs hierarchy. The higher needs, such as self-actualization, cannot be fulfilled until the lower levels of the hierarchy, such as physiology, safety, and belonging, are met. This indicates that teachers who help students improve their interpersonal relationships also contribute to students' potential to become motivated, engaged, and inspired.

The activities in this chapter provide a range of social-emotional strategies that teachers can use to help students develop relationships and realize the importance of gratitude, caring habits, and listening.

# Gratitude

Gratitude simply means being thankful and appreciative for the good things in one's life. Gratitude is closely tied to mental health and a positive outlook. Robert Emmons (2010), a lead researcher in the field of positive psychology and editor-in-chief of *The Journal of Positive Psychology*, explained the relationship this way:

> Depression has been shown to be strongly inversely related to gratitude. The more grateful a person is, the less depressed they are. The more depressed a person is, the less likely they are to go around feeling thankful for life. (p. 38)

Fortunately, students can learn gratitude. As students practice gratefulness, they tend to become more thoughtful, compassionate, caring toward others, and happy. In a particularly compelling study on gratitude, one group was asked to write down five unhappy events that occurred throughout the day; a second group was asked to record five events that occurred, specifying neither unhappy nor happy events; and the experiment group was asked to write down five things for which it felt gratitude. After ten weeks, according to the researchers' scale of well-being outcomes, the results showed that the gratitude condition had a 25 percent higher rating in overall life satisfaction when compared to the other groups. Emmons (2010) noted, "Participants in the gratitude condition reported considerably more satisfaction with their lives as a whole, felt more optimism about the upcoming week, and felt more connected with others than did participants in the control condition" (p. 33). The gratitude participants even slept more peacefully and exercised more than the participants in the other groups (Emmons, 2010).

It takes very little time to help students learn to make gratitude a regular part of each day, and just taking a few moments to reflect on the good in one's life can have positive long-term effects. While gratitude may seem like a simple tool, teachers should not overlook the effectiveness of gratitude as a mindfulness strategy. Here we describe three gratitude activities: (1) the ABCs of Gratitude, (2) the Ten-Finger Gratitude Exercise, and (3) letters of gratitude.

## The ABCs of Gratitude

The ABCs of Gratitude is an activity that helps students identify numerous things for which they are grateful. This activity can be used with students at any grade level. Here, we'll discuss three important elements to consider: (1) preparation, (2) essential learnings, and (3) directions.

### Preparation

The required materials for this activity are paper and writing utensils.

### Essential Learnings

Teaching students the following information about the benefits of gratitude will help them understand the reasons behind this activity.

- Gratitude, or being thankful, contributes to one's happiness.

- In a scientific study of gratitude, participants who regularly journaled about gratitude were happier, more energetic, and more optimistic than those who journaled about negative things or random events in their days (Emmons, 2010).

- Gratitude boosts overall health and may help people sleep better (Emmons, 2010).

### Directions

The ABCs of Gratitude uses the following four-step process.

1. Discuss with students what it means to feel grateful. Explain the scientific benefits of gratitude.

2. Ask students to write the letters A to Z on a sheet of paper in their journal, leaving enough space to write between each letter—perhaps one letter per line.

3. Invite students to write items for which they are grateful that correspond to each letter of the alphabet (see figure 6.1).

4. If time permits, ask students to share some of the things they wrote down or how they feel after thinking about the positive things in their lives.

| | |
|---|---|
| A—apples | N—Niall (my brother) |
| B—bees | O—oranges |
| C—cats | P—popcorn |
| D—donuts | Q—quizzes that get canceled |
| E—education | R—rain |
| F—forests | S—sleep |
| G—Grandma | T—toothbrushes |
| H—happiness | U—umbrellas |
| I—ice cream | V—vision |
| J—jokes that make me laugh | W—wind mills |
| K—kites | X—xylophones |
| L—lollipops | Y—yellow (my favorite color) |
| M—Mom | Z—Zach (my best friend) |

**Figure 6.1: Sample ABCs of Gratitude list.**

## The Ten-Finger Gratitude Exercise

The Ten-Finger Gratitude Exercise is a quick activity that asks students to count off ten things for which they are grateful. Students of any age can complete this exercise.

### Preparation

This activity requires no preparation or materials. Teachers can modify this activity as appropriate for their students or the time available; for example, teachers might ask elementary school students to come up with only five items instead of ten.

### Essential Learnings

Key purposes underlying this activity include the following.

- Small daily disciplines can greatly impact one's happiness and overall well-being.

- People can intentionally develop feelings of gratitude even when they don't start out feeling particularly grateful. This practice can develop habits of gratitude in day-to-day life.

- People can be grateful for even the little things in life.

- One should try to find new things to be grateful for. Reciting the same memorized list of things every day is unlikely to increase gratitude; instead, one should seek out varied things for which one feels gratitude.

### Directions

This activity includes three simple steps.

1. Discuss with students the benefits of gratitude.

2. Have students sit quietly and consider ten specific things, people, or events—one for each of the fingers on their hands—for which they can express their gratitude.

3. If time permits, invite students to share their thoughts about gratitude.

## Letters of Gratitude

Sending letters of gratitude is a more in-depth gratitude activity that invites students to write to a person who has positively influenced them. Showing gratitude in a written format helps clarify what it is students are truly grateful for and can help them practice acknowledging the positive effects of people in their lives. Additionally, the recipient generally feels gratitude upon receiving the letter, which can spawn further positivity and kindness. Such unambiguous expressions of thanks or acknowledgment are rare in many people's lives, so this activity can be deeply meaningful for both students and the recipients of their letters. This activity is most easily accomplished with students who can write independently, though teachers can adapt it for younger students as well.

### Preparation

For this activity, students will need paper, writing utensils, envelopes, stamps, and the addresses of the people to whom they are writing their letters. Some teachers might choose to include a note explaining the assignment with the letter, but it is also perfectly appropriate to send the letter alone. Teachers should give students thirty to forty-five minutes to write their first drafts, with the possibility of additional time later for editing and formatting final drafts.

### Essential Learnings

Use the following points to contextualize this activity for students.

- There are many people for whom one can be grateful.

- Sometimes people do not realize the difference they have made in another person's life unless that person lets them know.

- Gratitude contributes both to the happiness of the person giving thanks and to the happiness of the person receiving thanks.

### Directions

Teachers can use the following seven steps to write letters of gratitude with their classes.

1. Discuss with students the purpose of the letter.

2. Brainstorm some possible recipients together, such as a former teacher, a coach, a parent, or a grandparent.

3. Provide students with in-class time to draft their letters. Students may turn in their letters at the end of the first session for teachers to review.

4. After the first session, give students several days to locate an address for the recipient. Teachers may provide students with additional guidance if they are uncertain of how to go about getting a specific person's address.

5. In a second session, give students time to revise and edit their drafts. Teachers may also assist students with technical, content, or formatting questions at this time.

6. Demonstrate how to address an envelope.

7. As an optional step, students or teachers could write a brief note to include with the letter that explains the class project on gratitude.

## Caring Habits

Common behaviors in human interactions fall into two categories: (1) connecting habits that bring people closer together and (2) disconnecting habits that tear relationships apart. William Glasser (1998, 2006) encouraged teachers to interact with students without ever using the disconnecting habits. He stressed that the disconnecting habits are what teachers and parents often resort to when they are trying to externally control students. In contrast, he suggested that when people use connecting habits to try to build better relationships, they will find greater success in meeting their love and belonging needs. These habits can improve not only familial and student-teacher relationships but also peer-to-peer relationships among students. Table 6.1 lists the habits.

**Table 6.1: Connecting and Disconnecting Habits**

| Connecting Habits | Disconnecting Habits |
|---|---|
| Caring | Criticizing |
| Listening | Blaming |
| Supporting | Complaining |

Continued on next page →

| Connecting Habits | Disconnecting Habits |
|---|---|
| Contributing | Nagging |
| Encouraging | Threatening |
| Trusting | Punishing |
| Befriending | Rewarding people to control them |

By explicitly teaching and modeling the seven connecting habits and trying to eliminate the seven disconnecting habits from their interactions, teachers can help students develop the power to create meaningful, beneficial, and positive relationships. Learning and practicing the connecting habits, while avoiding the disconnecting habits, can additionally develop a supportive classroom and school culture that nurture feelings of belonging, trust, and safety among teachers and students. See the following two activities: (1) learning the caring habits and (2) practicing the caring habits.

## Learning the Caring Habits

Learning the caring habits involves understanding two types of behaviors: (1) those that build and strengthen relationships and (2) those that cause distrust, animosity, and conflict. This activity is appropriate for grades 3 and up, but teachers could adapt it for use in K–2 classrooms. Consider the following three elements: (1) preparation, (2) essential learnings, and (3) directions.

### Preparation

Teachers should develop a complete understanding of the connecting and disconnecting habits and be prepared to give examples before leading this activity. Teachers can adjust the length and depth of this activity based on student needs; the teacher's intention may be to simply make students aware of these concepts, or it could explain the habits in depth to develop a foundation for further activities, discussions, or classroom expectations.

### Essential Learnings

By the end of this activity, students should understand the following points.

- Connecting habits bring a person closer to others and include caring, listening, supporting, contributing, encouraging, trusting, and befriending.

- Disconnecting habits move a person away from others and include criticizing, blaming, complaining, nagging, threatening, punishing, and rewarding people to control them.

- People can consciously choose behaviors that will help create positive, caring relationships.

- It is possible to interact with others using only words and actions that are mutually helpful.

### Directions

This activity comprises the following six steps.

   1.  Invite students to sit in small groups.

2. Share the list of connecting habits with students, generally describe each habit, and then ask students to generate examples of behaviors that represent the different habits.

3. Ask them to consider why they believe these habits would help them connect with others.

4. Share the list of disconnecting habits with students, generally describe each habit, and then ask students to generate examples of behaviors that represent the different habits.

5. Ask them to consider why they believe these habits would damage relationships.

6. Call on students to share their responses to the different habits.

## Practicing the Caring Habits

Students can strengthen the relationships in their lives by practicing connecting habits. However, the first step in forming caring relationships is self-awareness. Students can't choose to enact new behaviors if they are unable to recognize connecting and disconnecting habits in themselves. Students also need to understand that people generally act a certain way because they believe it will help them meet specific needs or accomplish a goal. However, in some situations, the tactics people use to meet their needs interfere with others' happiness and needs. Students should be able to identify habits of behavior that can meet their needs without alienating or angering the people around them. Students can then self-evaluate and decide if the habits they utilize truly benefit themselves and others. After self-evaluating, the students can begin to correct negative habits of behavior by choosing more mutually beneficial strategies. Once students have chosen a specific habit, they must take steps toward changing their relationships by putting the connecting habits into action. Practicing the caring habits, which is appropriate for grades 5 and up, helps students internalize these concepts (Robbins, 2010, as cited in Suffield, 2012). Consider the following three elements: (1) preparation, (2) essential learnings, and (3) directions.

### Preparation

Teachers should allot twenty to thirty minutes for this activity, which will require two chairs, a set of yellow 8 x 10 cards with one of the seven caring habits printed on each (caring, listening, supporting, contributing, encouraging, trusting, and befriending), and a set of red 8 x 10 cards with one of the seven disconnecting habits printed on each (criticizing, blaming, complaining, nagging, threatening, punishing, and rewarding people to control them). Additionally, teachers may wish to develop several scenarios that students can act out, as well as prompts or scripts, before the day of the activity.

### Essential Learnings

Through this activity, students should come to understand the following information.

• Connecting habits bring a person closer to others and include caring, listening, supporting, contributing, encouraging, trusting, and befriending.

• Disconnecting habits move a person away from others and include criticizing, blaming, complaining, nagging, threatening, punishing, and rewarding people to control them.

• If people pause before they act, they can more consciously choose behaviors that will help them create positive, caring relationships.

### Directions

The following eleven-step process uses playacting to help students internalize the importance of using connecting habits.

1. Teach or review the meaning of the seven connecting habits and the seven disconnecting habits.

2. Hand out each of the red cards to seven students in the class. Hand out each of the yellow cards to seven students in the class. Have them hold the cards facedown for the time being.

3. Ask for two volunteers to act out a make-believe scenario about a friendship. Then, give the volunteers an age-appropriate scenario about a relationship that is not going well. For example, a teacher could ask students to act out a scenario between two teammates who are upset after losing a game, such as the following.

   • **Teammate 1:** I can't believe we lost! It's all because you missed that last goal. If you don't start making more goals, I am going to tell the coach to replace you with someone better.

   • **Teammate 2:** It was a hard shot, and the other team had a good goalie.

   • **Teammate 1:** Don't make excuses. You would be a better player if you stopped slacking off at practice. Now we will never make it to the state playoffs!

4. As the volunteers begin to share, the teacher invites the class to listen for any of the seven disconnecting habits.

5. After the scenario concludes, students should identify which habits they recognized and encourage the class member with the corresponding red card to stand up and move between the two students in the chairs. For instance, students might say that Teammate 1 from the sample scenario was threatening the other teammate when he or she said, "If you don't start making more goals, I am going to tell the coach to replace you with someone better."

6. Soon, several—if not all—students holding red cards will be between the two volunteers.

7. Ask the student acting out the disconnecting habits the following: "If each red card represents behavior that you are doing now, are the cards bringing you closer or further apart in this relationship?" Students with the red cards may sit back down after this step.

8. Then, ask the same volunteer student: "Are there any connecting habits you could try in this situation? What would you say instead to demonstrate these behaviors?"

9. The volunteer student will then describe some of the things he or she would say that relate to connecting habits. In the sample scenario, this could include phrases such as, "Thanks for making such a strong effort!" or "I know if we keep practicing we can improve before the next game!"

10. After the volunteer student finishes speaking, the rest of the class identifies which connecting habits they heard the volunteer student use. The students holding the cards for each habit can form a circle around the volunteers to symbolize the positive effects on the relationship.

11. Lead a brief discussion. Ask the student who was the recipient of the disconnecting habits, followed by the connecting habits, how he or she would feel in each scenario. Ask the other volunteer student to share how it felt using the two types of habits. Then in pairs or small groups, have students discuss what they witnessed and any applications for their own lives.

As a variation, teachers might perform this activity with multiple small groups, which allows more students to participate in the scenarios.

# Listening

Effective communication is about connecting with others. In order to truly listen, listeners must focus on what another person is saying, rather than thinking about what they will say next. Listening wholeheartedly is, therefore, closely linked to self-awareness, as listeners must be able to recognize when their minds wander and bring their attention back to the speaker. Focusing on a speaker can also help listeners respond thoughtfully instead of emotionally. This, in turn, can strengthen relationships and prevent unnecessary conflicts. Listening includes numerous components that may seem intuitive; however, by explicitly teaching components, teachers improve the likelihood that students will understand and implement effective listening across a variety of situations. The following sections describe two strategies that help students practice good listening skills: (1) effective listening and (2) Draw What I See.

## Effective Listening

Effective listening is an activity that allows students to experience what it feels like when they are not heard, as well as what it feels like for others to listen to and acknowledge them. Components of effective listening include using appropriate body language (such as turning one's shoulders and knees toward the speaker), maintaining eye contact, and setting aside distracting items. Listening also includes mental skills such as maintaining focus, tuning out distracting thoughts, and allowing the speaker to fully express him- or herself before responding. After completing this activity, students can compare each experience and explain why effective listening is an integral part of positive relationships. Consider the following three elements: (1) preparation, (2) essential learnings, and (3) directions.

### *Preparation*

This activity requires no materials. The completion of this activity will take approximately fifteen minutes.

### *Essential Learnings*

The following points list critical knowledge for students.

- Listening is not the same as hearing.

- Often, instead of truly listening to the speaker, people allow their minds to wander or start thinking about their responses.

- People can be mindful of others as they speak. This shows appreciation and respect for the speaker.

- Listening is a skill that can be developed and practiced.

- There are a number of effective listening skills, such as the following.

- Turning one's body toward the speaker

- Maintaining eye contact with the speaker

- Responding appropriately to the speaker with nods, smiles, and clarifying questions

- Shutting out distracting thoughts, much like in meditation

- Focusing on what the speaker is saying

- Trying not to one-up the speaker by telling a similar or more impressive story

- Setting aside distracting items, such as a cell phone

- Waiting to respond until the speaker is completely finished

### Directions

Teachers can use the following nine-step process to teach effective listening skills.

1. Ask students to think of a true story they would be willing to share with at least one other person in the room.

2. Assign or let students choose partners, then have students sit in chairs facing their partners.

3. Ask one student in each pair to listen to the other's story, trying to model *ineffective* listening habits. Give the speakers three minutes to talk.

4. Prompt students to share how it felt when they tried to communicate with someone who was disengaged.

5. Ask students to describe what qualities they would like to see from the listener.

6. Include several of the essential learnings as part of the discussion.

7. Instruct students to tell their stories again, except this time the listeners are to model *effective* listening practices. Give the speakers three minutes to talk.

8. Ask students to summarize how they felt as a speaker and as a listener when effective listening strategies were used and to describe any significant changes they noticed in their interactions.

9. Have students switch roles and repeat the process.

## Draw What I See

Draw What I See is an activity in which one student tries to replicate a picture based on the verbal descriptions of a partner. This helps students develop the skills of listening to directions and communicating effectively. It is appropriate for all grades, provided that the complexity of the pictures is appropriate for students' abilities.

### Preparation

For this activity, the teacher will want to find images ahead of time that one student can describe to another. For example, teachers could use basic shapes for grades K–1, while a picture of a baseball diamond with two trees nearby would be appropriate for grades 2–5. As students mature into grades

6–12, teachers can use more complex, abstract pictures. In addition to one picture for each student (pictures can repeat within the class, but within pairs each student should have a different image), the class will need paper and writing utensils. This activity takes fifteen to thirty minutes depending on the complexity of the picture.

### *Essential Learnings*

- Listening is a skill that students can learn and improve upon.

- Listening takes effort and energy.

- Listening to others is courteous, as well as informative.

### *Directions*

1. Divide the class into pairs of students. Give students one picture each, and tell them not to share their pictures with their partners.

2. Tell students that they are going to describe their pictures to their partners without naming the objects in the picture. Rather, they can only tell their partners where to place their writing utensils and how far to draw in which direction. Model what this might sound like: "Start with your pen in the bottom right corner. Draw a diagonal line about four inches long moving toward the top left corner. Now draw over to the left about two inches straight across and then straight down almost to the bottom of the paper."

3. Have students decide which partner will be the talker first and which will be the listener. Tell the first talkers that they will have five to seven minutes (or whatever length of time is appropriate) to describe their pictures to their partners.

4. After time is up, have the listeners share their artwork with the talkers and compare it to the original.

5. Ask pairs to discuss what ideas they have to better communicate the drawings.

6. Have partners switch roles. Give the students talking second the same time limit as the first and have students share and discuss afterward.

7. If time allows, elicit responses in a whole-class debrief. Here are some possible questions.

   - "Was it easier to give directions or to listen?"

   - "What worked well? What was frustrating?"

   - "How closely did your drawing resemble the original?"

   - "What did you learn from this activity?"

## Summary

Positive interactions make a powerful difference in students' lives. Instead of simply expecting that they already have these important prosocial behaviors, it is important that teachers take the time to teach, model, and reinforce these habits. This chapter described several strategies related to gratitude, caring habits, and listening that teachers can use to introduce prosocial behaviors in the classroom. Positive interactions among teachers and students contribute to a caring, supportive classroom atmosphere and a safe school culture. Strengthening students' social-emotional skills also enhances their abilities to carry prosocial skills into adulthood as parents, employees, and civic leaders. The next chapter delineates strategies for incorporating the concepts and ideas from the previous chapters into a classroom or school and offers specific advice, cautions, and helpful tips.

# Chapter 6: Comprehension Questions

1. How does mindfulness cause positive interactions?

2. What effects does regularly practicing gratitude have?

3. How do connecting and disconnecting habits affect relationships?

4. List four effective listening habits.

Chapter 7

# STEPS FOR IMPLEMENTING MINDFULNESS IN YOUR CLASSROOM OR SCHOOL

Although this chapter includes a step-by-step process for bringing mindfulness to a classroom or school, it is important to note that teachers and instructors should feel free to personalize these strategies to fit their unique situations and goals. Teachers can incorporate mindfulness informally or formally, on a small or large scale. For example, some teachers may wish to use some of this book's individual strategies on an occasional basis; perhaps they find that the breathing strategies help students refocus after recess or that the positive interaction strategies are a solution to classroom behavior issues. However, some educators may want to incorporate mindfulness into their schools and classrooms in a more consistent and defined manner. Those teachers and schools looking for a more formal, systematic program can use this chapter as a guide. A schoolwide program will require more intentional preparation and execution. For either occasional or schoolwide implementation of mindfulness, this chapter offers helpful suggestions and tips.

Next, we will discuss the five important steps to implement mindfulness: (1) educating yourself, (2) educating school leaders, (3) educating parents, (4) educating students, (5) developing a classroom plan, (6) measuring results, and (7) implementing a schoolwide mindfulness program.

## Educating Yourself

For people who are new to mindfulness, it is important to consider adding mindful practices to daily life in order to experience the benefits firsthand. This firsthand experience creates a more complete understanding that enables effective implementation of mindfulness in schools and classrooms. Further, the teacher's own ongoing practice allows for more authentic implementation with students.

There are many resources available for those who wish to deepen their knowledge of mindfulness. Numerous websites and a plethora of research articles cover this topic, and nearly every bookstore and library will have books available on the topic of mindfulness. Teachers may even consider including a resource, such as this book, in an instructional-group book study to develop a common understanding and vocabulary concerning mindfulness. Magazines are also a useful way to gain a broad perspective of mindfulness. *Mindful* is one such publication that offers both digital and print versions. Additional books, magazines, and other resources on mindfulness are listed in appendix B (page 107).

Another approach to educating oneself on mindfulness is to enroll in a course. The most beneficial courses for implementation in the classroom are those that are designed specifically for schools. Research-based programs include but are not limited to Mindful Schools, MindUP, and Calm Classroom. An individual teacher or a group of staff members might complete a course such as these prior to using mindfulness in a school or classroom. Courses are offered in a variety of ways, including online and face-to-face. Appendix B also includes a list of mindfulness education programs.

Many cities and towns have mindfulness and meditation groups that meet regularly. Participating in groups helps practitioners maintain a disciplined practice and learn from like-minded individuals. No matter the platform, gaining a broad understanding of mindfulness, as well as practicing it regularly, is an essential key to successful implementation in a classroom or school.

## Educating School Leaders

For a mindfulness program to be successful, it is imperative that school leaders have some level of understanding and buy-in. Although mindfulness training has gained a tremendous amount of acceptance in the mainstream, some groups resist its use because it is not a traditional practice in American education or because of its roots in Buddhism and Hinduism (Wilson, 2014). Because well-intentioned parents may bring their concerns to the attention of administrators, these administrators would benefit from a strong knowledge base regarding the science and research on mindfulness in schools (see chapter 1, page 3).

Another reason school leaders should engage in mindfulness education is because it helps create a sense of consistency and community across the school. For this reason, the school principal's treatment of students in disciplinary or everyday interactions should ideally parallel the goals of mindfulness training. As an example, a school principal who uses disconnecting habits, such as threats or criticism, instead of connecting habits, such as listening and encouragement, will contradict the lessons students learn in their mindfulness instruction. In contrast, when the principal uses mindfulness-related phrases and vocabulary or joins in activities, such as a brief meditation or mindful nature walk, students may deem these activities more valuable.

Depending on their level of involvement, the education for administrative teams can vary. At the very least, administrators would benefit from reading a book that provides an overview of the research, science, and techniques that make up mindfulness. This knowledge is essential for consistent communication with students, staff, parents, and the community. We also recommend a book study with the leadership team and interested teachers. If school leaders intend to provide significant support, then they might seek a similar level of education as teachers who plan to lead mindfulness, including online or in-person trainings, consistent practice of mindfulness, and ongoing reading.

In the case of schoolwide implementation, administrator training is not only beneficial but necessary. In order to plan trainings, create an action plan, and communicate with staff and parents, an administrator needs a comprehensive understanding of mindfulness. Ideally, school leaders will study and practice mindfulness for several months before leading a full-scale implementation.

## Educating Parents

Having parents on board is helpful when implementing mindfulness in a classroom or school, especially in the case of a formal program. When parents understand mindfulness and its benefits, they are more likely to accept it. Teaching parents about the need for mindfulness is a good first step. If parents are able to embrace the idea of mindfulness, their modeling at home can compound the beneficial effects for students.

[DATE]


Dear Parents and Guardians,

I would like to cordially invite you to an informational meeting to discuss a need that students in our modern society are facing—a need for peace of mind. Students of all ages are facing much more stresses than most of us realize. With that in mind, I would like to share with you the topic of *mindfulness training*. Mindfulness teaches specific skills to help students stay focused, be aware, have empathy, and learn how to respect themselves as well as others.

At [NAME OF SCHOOL] we are working on self-regulation and mindfulness skills. The positive impact of mindfulness has been demonstrated in personal practice, schools, as well as extensively in the fields of medicine and psychology. Mindfulness work in education is expanding rapidly. It has been shown to increase focus and concentration, decrease stress and anxiety, improve impulse control, and increase empathy. The Mindful Schools curriculum specifically has been studied in classrooms and found to significantly improve students' attention spans, calmness, self-control, self-care, and respect for others. Medical doctors, psychologists, and counselors are recommending mindfulness to their patients. Schools are answering students' high levels of anxiety and stress with mindfulness practices.

This meeting will explain in greater depth why mindfulness is a valuable tool for our students. Please note, parents always reserve the right to have their child(ren) opt out. During this meeting, I will also be sharing with you the most recent data from our students' Youth Risk Behavior Survey, Prevention Needs Assessment, and behavior data. These data speak not about children in other communities but in our own community. There is evidence that our students would benefit from what mindfulness training can bring to those who practice it.

Please join us in learning more about the benefits of mindfulness training for your child.

What: [NAME OF EVENT]

When: [DATE AND TIME]

Where: [LOCATION]


In closing, thank you for your careful consideration of this opportunity to learn more and give us your opinion. We value what you have to say, and we value the well-being of your child.


Yours in education,

[YOUR NAME]

**Figure 7.1: Sample letter to parents.**

The process of educating parents can take a variety of forms, depending on their interest. An informational meeting for interested parents is a good first step (a sample invitation letter is shown in figure 7.1. During the informational meeting, it is important to share research that supports mindfulness for students. Parents may also benefit from a list of resources that can help them independently learn more about the topic. A book study for parents, utilizing this book or one similar, is recommended for those parents eager to learn more about mindfulness practice. When parents model at home what students are working on in school, it encourages students' acceptance and practice of mindfulness activities.

Invite and include parents in mindfulness trainings or events whenever possible. It may be valuable to provide parents with a calendar highlighting upcoming trainings and classroom mindfulness activities. Allowing parents to visit classrooms during mindfulness lessons can also help alleviate apprehension and create a transparent and inviting school culture.

Many parents will likely appreciate that the school is teaching social-emotional skills to their children that support positive changes in their children's behaviors at home. However, not everyone will accept the idea of mindfulness. Thus, it is imperative to communicate with parents early and often as to the intent, format, and content of mindfulness training. Let parents know they have the right to opt their child out of mindfulness training at any time and that their student will have quiet time to read, draw, or journal while other students participate in mindfulness. Ideally, encourage parents to allow their child to try mindfulness training a few times before making the decision to opt out.

## Educating Students

Teachers can introduce mindfulness to students in numerous ways. One method is to begin by sharing the definition of mindfulness and explaining the benefits in student-friendly terminology. Table 7.1 shows student-friendly definitions of mindfulness and its benefits. Students might record these or write their own definitions of each term during an initial lesson.

**Table 7.1: Student-Friendly Definitions of Mindfulness Terms and Phrases**

| Terms and Phrases | Student-Friendly Definition |
| --- | --- |
| Mindfulness | Paying attention to what's going on in our minds and in the world |
| Emotional regulation | Being better able to control outbursts |
| Increased focus | Feeling less distracted |
| Longer attention span | Paying attention for longer periods of time |
| Reduced rumination | Spending less time obsessing about bad things |
| Greater receptivity to new ideas | Being open-minded |
| Reduced stress and anxiety | Feeling calm |
| Faster rebound from negative thoughts and feelings | Not letting negative thoughts get you down |
| More thoughtful reactions to stimuli | Thinking before you act |
| Increased compassion | Being kind to everyone |
| Better self-control | Sitting still even when it's hard to do so |
| Less reactive | Taking time to think about what you'll do next |
| Better executive function | Making smarter decisions |
| Increased optimism | Having a happier outlook on life |
| Higher working memory capacity | Being better able to learn |

| Improved emotional intelligence | Better understanding your own and other people's emotions |
| --- | --- |
| Decreased depression | Not feeling sad as often |
| Better immune system | Not getting sick as often |

Another method for introducing mindfulness to students is to provide them with a mindfulness experience. The simpler mindfulness activities such as nature walks or box breathing are very accessible even to those who know nothing about mindfulness. Teachers can take students through an appropriate activity and then have them evaluate how they felt before and after the experience. From there, teachers can introduce the term *mindfulness* and its definition and ask students to come up with a definition and then post it in the classroom. Teachers may also wish to share a few of the benefits of mindfulness and, depending on the receptivity of the students, choose another activity to try out a few days later. Before more extensive mindfulness activities, it may also be useful to revisit the definition of mindfulness and describe additional reasons for practicing mindfulness.

As much as teachers and school leadership may believe in the transformative power of mindfulness, it is important not to force this practice onto students. Some students and parents will not approve of any type of mindfulness. Also, it is important to note that mindfulness training is effective for most students but not necessarily for all. From the outset, teachers and administrators should explain clearly that they understand that mindfulness may not be right for everyone and that students will not be forced to participate. However, teachers should encourage unsure students to give mindfulness practice a try before passing judgment. If they remain uncomfortable after a few activities, offer them other choices, such as reading, journaling, working on homework, drawing, or other silent activities.

## Developing a Classroom Plan

Sometimes, an individual teacher may be interested in implementing a formal mindfulness program in his or her classroom without the guidance of a school- or districtwide plan. Perhaps the teacher knows about the benefits of mindfulness from personal experience or has read research about the topic and feels it would help develop students' social-emotional skills. Whatever the teacher's motivations may be, it is generally not necessary to wait for schoolwide implementation. The following eight-step plan serves as a guide for adopting mindfulness in a classroom.

1. Practice mindfulness every day for several months. To begin, we suggest incorporating mindful meditation into one's routine for five to ten minutes each day. When this becomes a habit, practice an additional mindfulness activity such as mindful eating, belly breathing, or staying on task.

2. Read a variety of resources related to mindfulness (see appendix B, page 107). Building one's knowledge base regarding mindfulness is key to successful implementation in the classroom. For example, some sources may include unique techniques and strategies that are particularly effective for the situations and needs of specific students or classrooms. Teachers can also find their own resources by examining the reference sections of especially helpful articles, books, and digital sources.

3. Attend mindfulness trainings or take an online course (see appendix B). Trainings vary in price and time commitment, so teachers should be able to find something that fits their

individual needs. The step-by-step presentation of materials in an instructional setting can help solidify one's understanding of both the reasons to practice and strategies to develop mindfulness.

4. Express a guiding intention or purpose in a sentence or two. Teachers should be aware of their intent before beginning to teach mindfulness to students. One example of an intention statement might be, "My intent in teaching mindfulness to my students is to provide them with tools for handling the stresses of life, to help them make choices aligned with their own values, and to aid them in improving their overall well-being."

5. Create an action plan. An action plan helps teachers clarify the steps for successful classroom implementation. One method of developing an action plan could involve SMART goals, which are discussed in greater detail next.

6. Discuss the science behind mindfulness with the building principal. Depending on the openness of the community, a discussion with the superintendent may also be necessary. If administrators are less than supportive, it would be wise for classroom teachers to focus on emotional intelligence skills or on stress reduction and breathing techniques, both of which are often more easily accepted by administrators.

7. With administrator approval, send a letter home to parents. This letter should begin by detailing the ways students can benefit from mindfulness and the science that supports mindfulness. The letter should also specify approximately how much class time will be allocated to mindfulness. Further, the letter should communicate parents' and students' right to opt out of participation as well as an invitation for parents to observe or participate in mindfulness training. Figure 7.1 (page 85) depicts an example.

8. Have a class meeting about the reasons for mindfulness training before beginning. Allow students to give input as to which mindfulness activity or program might best suit their class. With students' input, set up parameters for those students choosing to opt out.

As teachers begin to work toward implementation of a mindfulness program, they may want to consider using a series of SMART (strategic and specific, measurable, attainable, results oriented, and time bound) goals to structure their action plan. Although SMART goals are not new (see O'Neill & Conzemius, 2006), they are worth mentioning here. SMART goals as they apply to mindfulness involve the following elements.

- **Strategic and specific:** Describe the exact task or activity. For example, one of the teacher's first goals may be to have a conversation with the building principal about the purposes of mindfulness to share his or her intent.

- **Measurable:** Measurable goals are ones that show growth or lack of growth over time. The easiest way to make a goal measurable is with a number. Without a number, a goal may be well-intentioned but not measurable. Take this example of a nonmeasurable goal for comparison: "Students will be safer on our playground." Although the intent is sound, how would one know if this goal has been reached? By simply adding numbers, goals can become measureable: "At the end of this semester, we will have had twelve fewer safety incidents on the playground than we did last semester."

- **Attainable:** Create a goal that teachers or students can reasonably achieve. For example, while teachers likely hope that there will never be any injuries on the playground, this is probably not a realistic goal. In contrast, the previously stated goal of decreasing safety incidents by twelve is attainable. Attaining simpler goals can also fuel motivation to accomplish bigger goals and serve as steps toward more transformative changes.

- **Results oriented:** Gather evidence to gauge the results, or lack thereof. Teachers should develop methods for evaluating progress toward a goal. For instance, teachers who want to see improvement in playground safety could record data on behavior incidents, trips to the nurse, and so on.

- **Time bound:** Establish a deadline for each goal. We advise setting due dates that are short term (up to one year) rather than long term to maintain staff and student motivation. Create further SMART goals as specific goals are met.

Figure 7.2 depicts a sample action plan that illustrates the use of SMART goals. Note that each goal is specific and measurable, as is the person (or people) responsible for carrying out said tasks.

| Specific Goal | Measurement of Success | Person Responsible | Resources Needed | Date for Completion |
|---|---|---|---|---|
| Research various types of mindfulness programs and activities. | A list of top three programs or activities in order with rationale for their selections | Classroom teacher | Money for piloting programs; time to read and pilot; time for research; books and program lists | Four weeks from today |
| Select which type of mindfulness programming to implement. | A selected program or a list of activities that we will choose to pilot | Teacher working with the school counselor | Time to meet with the school counselor | Eight weeks from today |
| Recruit two additional staff members to participate in mindfulness training. | Two staff members have committed to participating | School counselor and teacher | $125 per person for mindfulness training online; time for face-to-face discussions of learning | February 15 of this school year |
| Send an informational letter to parents. | Parents receive letter | Teacher | Postage; parents' addresses | One month prior to implementation with students |
| Host a parent information night. | Feedback from parents collected via one-on-one conversations and a digital or print survey | Teacher Principal School counselor | Refreshments; materials and time to create handouts and surveys | Three weeks prior to implementation |
| Implementation of program in three classrooms | Documentation of implementation and student feedback | Three teachers | Time to implement | By March 15 of this year |

**Figure 7.2: Sample action plan.**

## Measuring Results

There are many ways to measure results. Teachers need to first consider what they hope to achieve by incorporating mindfulness practice into their classrooms. For instance, they may envision a classroom rife with confident, calm, happy, compassionate, attentive students who are committed to their learning and well-being. Statements of intention teachers wrote (page 88) are useful here. Again, to make this goal more concrete, feasible, and measurable, the teacher should follow the SMART goal method or one similar. Once the teacher has established a goal, the teacher should regularly gather information that measures progress.

Using survey data is one method for attaining feedback on the success of mindfulness practices. Teachers could create a brief survey that asks students how often they feel a certain way, such as happy, anxious, or depressed, or how frequently they perform certain behaviors. Teachers could then administer this survey before and after mindfulness training to determine its effect on student well-being. For K–2 students, teachers may read survey items and use images of smiling faces, neutral faces, and frowning faces to represent possible responses. While studying initial survey results, it is best to choose one or two areas to improve through the use of mindfulness.

Another method for measurement is using quantifiable data. Perhaps a teacher's goal is to increase students' ability to focus on their reading. This can be quantified by preassessing how many minutes the entire class stays on task during silent reading time. After the preassessment, the teacher can utilize one of the mindfulness strategies that he or she believes will help students focus, such as mindfulness meditation (page 7), right before reading time. The teacher can do this for several weeks and then reassess the number of minutes students are able to focus. While other variables besides mindfulness may contribute to the results, the teacher can still study results with some confidence that the intervention (mindfulness meditation) likely contributed to their ability to focus. Teachers can also study specific interventions by trying them with some classes and not with others and comparing the results.

Another important part of measuring results is to maintain a documentation guideline (shown in figure 7.3). This type of guideline records valuable feedback to the teacher as to what worked from the teacher's and students' viewpoints and can inform future changes.

| Name of Mindfulness Activity or Program | Teacher's Overall Impression on a 1–10 Scale | Teacher Comments | Students' Average Overall Impression on a 1–10 Scale | Sample of Student Comments |
|---|---|---|---|---|
| Box breathing | 9 | "Easy to use" <br> "Not time intensive" <br> "Calmed the students" | 8 | "It's okay." <br> "I like the way it quieted the classroom." <br> "Boring" <br> "Let's keep it." |
| Mindfulness meditation | 8 | "Class was much more relaxed following just five minutes." <br> "I need more training; not sure what to do with the kids who don't like it or don't want to do it." <br> "Is it okay to close my eyes?" | 7 | "Peaceful, relaxing" <br> "Boring" <br> "The class felt kinder afterward." <br> "Let's keep doing this." |

| Eating a Raisin | 5 | "I need more confidence."<br><br>"The students didn't understand the purpose."<br><br>"Perhaps I need more training or didn't lead it right." | 3 | "It made me hungry."<br><br>"Stupid activity"<br><br>"Why only one raisin?"<br><br>"I don't understand the purpose of slowing down."<br><br>"I liked the 'Rush and rush until life's no fun' song that you played." |

**Figure 7.3: Sample documentation guideline.**

## Implementing a Schoolwide Mindfulness Program

Some schools may be ready for a more comprehensive approach to mindfulness. A schoolwide mindfulness program is when staff members, school administrators, and parents have a common understanding of the benefits of mindfulness and are willing to invest the time and resources to bringing mindfulness to students. Generally, a schoolwide mindfulness program requires at least a principal who is fully invested in mindfulness training. In cases where the principal is one of the major proponents, mindfulness programs—although perhaps not accepted by all—are often more readily received schoolwide. Whatever the case, gaining the support of the building leader is necessary for a successful schoolwide approach to mindfulness.

The benefits of a schoolwide approach are many. In a large-scale mindfulness program, students throughout the school have shared goals such as self-regulation, compassion, focus, attention, and calmness. They also hear shared vocabulary terms and phrases such as *mindful walking*, *belly breathing*, *mindful meditation*, and *body scans*. When students hear these common expectations and phrases and see them modeled throughout the school, on the playground, in the halls, in the lunchroom, and in the principal's office, their capacity to internalize mindfulness increases.

As part of a schoolwide action plan or strategic plan, school leaders or teachers need certain components. The following sections describe four aspects that leaders should consider in the planning process: (1) forming a guiding team, (2) gathering input and sharing information, (3) implementing the program successfully, and (4) allowing teachers to opt out.

### Forming a Guiding Team

A guiding team is a focused and committed group of people whose purpose is to explore, lead, and support a schoolwide initiative. As a district or school begins the process of incorporating mindfulness training, it is imperative to establish a guiding team. The membership of the guiding team, at its best, includes varied stakeholders: teachers, counselors, parents, community members, support staff, and age-appropriate students. Having a variety of stakeholders allows for representation of many perspectives, which ensures that decisions the team makes will not only focus on student achievement but also on the improvement of students' well-being and community culture as a whole.

The inclusive approach may be the best way to build a guiding team. Begin by inviting all staff members in the school to the first organizational meeting. This may result in a huge turnout, or it may only attract a handful of highly interested staff members. Also invite indifferent and even opposed staff members to attend. Participation from staff members who may be less supportive of a specific vision can be helpful in the planning process because they may provide a unique perspective that challenges the team to think more carefully about what best suits a school and community's unique needs. Additionally, by making the discussion inclusive, staff members can move past possibly unfounded perceptions of mindfulness and work together toward concrete next steps. In this first organizational meeting, staff can decide who will continue as permanent members of the guiding team. They can also decide when to include other stakeholders, including parents and age-appropriate students, and their roles in the guiding team.

Questions such as the following can help focus this first meeting.

- Why is it important to focus on the whole child, including social, emotional, and physical needs, as well as cognitive skills?

- What kind of learning environment best supports the whole child?

- What kind of learning environment do we want for our students?

- What are the emotional needs of our students?

- How can we help our students feel a sense of calm and belonging?

- What are the data telling us in relation to students' safety? Student absences? Office referrals? School culture?

- In what areas of student behavior, safety, and inclusion would we like to see improvements?

- What do students need in order to feel safe and at home in our learning environment?

Using the guiding questions, the guiding team may want to consider writing a one-sentence purpose statement to focus its work. An example statement could be, "The purpose of our Well-Being Focus Group is to provide students with tools and strategies to strengthen their emotional well-being and overall health."

After crafting a purpose statement, the next step for the guiding team is to write an action plan (page 88). Again, we recommend that the team use the SMART goal format (or one similar) as a guide. The action plan should be comprehensive and include actionable items such as how to include and inform parents and students, what training teachers will need, which books will guide the learning, what other resources teachers require, and specific deadlines. The action plan should also be very specific about whose role it is to accomplish tasks. This clarity will prove useful when moving forward. Again, it is critical to start with small, attainable goals. The guiding team might consider training a group of teachers willing to pilot mindfulness as the first actionable item; if that step seems too large, the team could begin with a voluntary book study on mindfulness. Over time, the capacity of a program will grow, and more significant steps can be taken toward schoolwide implementation.

## Gathering Input and Sharing Information

Gathering input and sharing information are essential to successful schoolwide implementation. An open, transparent process will bring clarity and promote synergy between various viewpoints. Including parents is especially critical when implementing a schoolwide initiative, and typically results in a richer, more in-depth program than one led by only a few stakeholders. Here are a few steps to consider.

- Send an informational letter to all parents.

- Have a mindfulness training or information night for parents.

- Teach the science behind mindfulness.

- Invite parents to attend mindfulness sessions with their child.

When gathering input and planning, try not to let one voice overpower the guiding team. Find strategies to include input from all members. Members may want to consider meeting in small groups to formulate strategies and ideas and then taking input from each group.

The guiding team should consider sharing the documentation with a larger group of stakeholders and seeking their input before making a final decision. It is also important to genuinely listen and consider the opinions of outside stakeholders; this process has little purpose if leaders have an inflexible point of view about results or next steps.

## Implementing the Program Successfully

Successful implementation of a schoolwide mindfulness program takes some foresight. Each community and school has its own unique needs; however, the advice we provide here is worth considering.

Start slowly and begin with reasonable first steps. If the guiding team has an interest in a specific program, pilot it in a few teachers' classrooms. As teachers implement various strategies, the guiding team can collect feedback about different practices' effectiveness from both teachers and students. The guiding team should also take note of any difficulties or resistance pilot teachers face during implementation. At the end of the pilot program, the guiding team can evaluate its success and any changes it should make before further program utilization.

It is also important to work closely with the community and parents. Some communities may be more apprehensive about a schoolwide mindfulness program. In situations like this, asking teachers on the guiding team to pilot one or two of the less controversial activities, such as box breathing, may prove beneficial. Use quiet reflection periods as an informal type of meditation. Even when using formal meditation, beginning with short periods (perhaps five minutes) eases the transition.

Further, it is imperative that all teachers who are training students in mindfulness receive proper training. Schools wouldn't expect teachers to teach a foreign language unless the teachers had credentials, language fluency, and an understanding of the associated culture. The same is true for mindfulness. Teachers must learn and experience mindfulness to teach it with authenticity and authority.

We recommend that stakeholders give an activity a three-week trial period before adopting or dismissing it. When activities are new, they may feel awkward at first. As with anything new, it takes practice and repetition to reach a comfort level.

## Allowing Teachers to Opt Out

When teachers embrace mindfulness, it validates the practice to students. However, it is not realistic to assume or expect that all teachers will accept mindfulness. Many teachers who are resistant at first will become more accepting once they understand that mindfulness is a psychological practice based in the science of reducing stress and providing tools for self-regulation and focus. As data show improvement in students' attitudes, attention, self-regulation, social skills, and behavior, reluctant teachers may eventually accept mindfulness. However, some teachers, no matter how much training or evidence they receive, will have concerns about mindfulness as a form of religious practice or have other reasons for not wanting to lead it in their classrooms. Staff members should have the right to opt out, but that does not mean their students' needs can be ignored. Hence, if mindfulness training is a core program for all students in a school or district, it will be necessary to provide a different leader than the classroom teacher.

Flexibility is key with staff members, but even reluctant teachers should be respectful of mindfulness practices. Teachers who opt out of mindfulness should never express their negative opinions to students, either directly or indirectly. If another educator comes into the classroom to conduct an activity, the teacher must contribute to the calm, mindful environment. If the teacher intends to complete other tasks, such as grading papers, while the activity is occurring, it may be most appropriate for the teacher to leave the classroom so as not to distract students.

## Summary

This chapter discussed several key areas to consider when implementing mindfulness programs on a small or large scale, including educating various stakeholders (including yourself, school leaders, parents, and students), developing a program for an individual classroom, measuring results, and developing a program for an entire school. It is important to customize mindfulness programs to the specific situation. Individual teachers can successfully utilize mindfulness activities within their classrooms and reap great results with students. Schoolwide and even districtwide implementation works as well but takes considerably more planning and input for success. Regardless of the scale of implementation, preparation is necessary. Training, thoughtful planning, and a clear understanding of the purpose of mindfulness activities are essential. Gathering input and disseminating information are also necessary, even for a classroom teacher. Despite the required work done up front, the benefits to students in the present and in their futures make all of the time, effort, and resources worth the investment.

# Chapter 7: Comprehension Questions

1. What stakeholder groups must you inform or educate when implementing mindfulness in a classroom or school?

2. What are the main action steps for a teacher implementing mindfulness in his or her classroom?

3. What are the benefits to schoolwide mindfulness programs?

4. Why should teachers and students be allowed to opt out?

# EPILOGUE

We know students are facing immense anxiety, sadness, stress, and worry. This book identifies these issues and posits that schools have an opportunity to step in and make a difference by directly teaching students how to manage emotions and stress. *Cultivating Mindfulness in the Classroom* supports the notion that mindfulness is a highly effective, low-cost strategy that helps students meet their needs for psychological well-being in the present and in their futures. Instead of simply telling students to be kind, calm down, keep their hands to themselves, and pay attention, this book offers tools for teaching students *how* to do those things. In addition, it provides guidance for educators who wish to implement a comprehensive mindfulness program in their classrooms or schools. As educators begin to incorporate these ideas and strategies in their classrooms and schools, we believe they will see a change in their students' abilities to control their emotions, self-regulate, and focus. Most important, students' self-concepts, relationships, and senses of efficacy will begin to improve, allowing them to face challenges and live more happy and fulfilling lives.

# APPENDIX A

# ANSWERS TO COMPREHENSION QUESTIONS

# Answers to Chapter 2: Comprehension Questions

1. *How does stress negatively impact the body?*

   During the fight-or-flight response and during prolonged stress, one's cortisol levels, heart rate, and blood pressure are all elevated. In the short term, one is likely to become physically and mentally exhausted more quickly. Over time, stress leads to increased risk of physical health problems such as heart disease, as well as mental health problems like depression.

2. *Why are breathing exercises useful in the classroom?*

   Breathing exercises reduce stress and lower one's heart rate. They also increase blood flow, which brings more oxygen to the brain, increasing one's ability to learn.

3. *How does the glitter jar activity help students visualize nonstop thinking?*

   The glitter in the water represents nonstop thinking; it swirls around and obscures the water like intrusive thoughts obscure clear thinking. When the glitter settles to the bottom of the jar, it represents times when the mind is calm and clear.

4. *According to research, what positive effects does nature have on people?*

   Research has found that interacting with nature helps lower one's stress levels. It improves a person's general quality of life. Studies have even shown that the presence of nature reduces crime rates in an area and helps people heal faster after surgery.

# Answers to Chapter 3: Comprehension Questions

1. *How does mindfulness practice improve attention?*

   Mindfulness activities involve focusing on what is happening in the present moment, rather than thinking about the past or the future. Mindfulness teaches practitioners to notice when they have become distracted and to gently bring their attention back to the task at hand. Attention is a skill that can be practiced and improved, and mindfulness activities often include direct practice of this skill.

2. *Why is practicing mindful attention important for students?*

   When students can mindfully pay attention and focus for longer, they are more engaged in school and can attend to instruction for sustained periods. They are less likely to get distracted and miss important information. Mindfulness also helps moderate extreme attention tendencies such as obsessiveness, hyperactivity, lack of concentration, and apathy.

3. *How does the Eating a Raisin activity help students practice attention?*

   Eating is something that many people do without thinking or paying attention. This activity asks students to eat a raisin very, very slowly, almost as if they have never done it before. They also consciously take in information from all five senses. In these ways, students practice attending to even the most mundane activities.

4. *Why can technology be detrimental to attention?*

   While technology does have its place in life and in education, it can also be extremely distracting. Devices such as cell phones tend to emit a constant stream of stimuli that interrupt any attempt at sustained focus on a task. This causes people to task-switch—to go back and forth between two tasks, or between a task and a distraction—which leads to decreased efficiency and increased errors.

# Answers to Chapter 4: Comprehension Questions

1. *What is emotional control?*

   Emotional control is the ability to notice one's emotions and respond to events thoughtfully. In other words, a person who has strong emotional control recognizes and acknowledges his or her feelings, but does not let emotion drive action. This is especially important in challenging situations.

2. *Describe each phase of the awareness, analysis, and choice process.*

   Awareness involves noticing a feeling and trying to determine the cause behind it. Analysis means thinking of the various options for responding to whatever caused the emotion and predicting the outcome for each option. The choice phase is when the person picks the option that he or she thinks will lead to the best or most desirable outcome.

3. *Why is optimism important to emotional control?*

   People are naturally more likely to get swept up by negative feelings. For this reason, learning to have a more positive outlook on life improves one's emotional resilience.

# Answers to Chapter 5: Comprehension Questions

1. *Define self-concept, self-efficacy, and self-esteem.*

   Self-concept is one's overall view of oneself and one's abilities. Self-efficacy is the perception that one is competent and able to achieve one's goals. Self-esteem is one's sense of value or self-worth.

2. *How does body language affect self-concept?*

   Body language can improve self-concept by making a person feel more confident. It is difficult to have a negative self-concept when one uses confident or assertive body language. Body language also influences hormones—confident, expansive posture increases testosterone and decreases cortisol, making the person feel and act more powerful.

3. *What is self-compassion?*

   Self-compassion, at its simplest, means being nice to oneself. In practice, people can approach this by attempting to treat themselves as they would treat a loved one, such as a close friend or family member. To be self-compassionate, a person must accept his or her own imperfections and avoid harsh judgments about him- or herself.

# Answers to Chapter 6: Comprehension Questions

1. *How does mindfulness cause positive interactions?*

   Because mindfulness reduces impulsiveness, it allows people to choose kind, positive responses to those around them. It improves social-emotional skills, such as empathy, so that people know how to be compassionate and friendly to others. Overall, it helps create a culture of respect and belonging.

2. *What effects does regularly practicing gratitude have?*

   Regularly practicing gratitude increases one's happiness and general satisfaction with life. It also tends to make people more optimistic about the future and even helps them sleep better.

3. *How do connecting and disconnecting habits affect relationships?*

   Connecting habits build better relationships because they involve interactions that are mutually beneficial. They create feelings of trust and belonging. Disconnecting habits break down relationships because one person is attempting to gain control over the other. This causes conflict and creates a power imbalance.

4. *List four effective listening habits.*

   Effective listening habits include turning one's body toward the speaker; maintaining eye contact with the speaker; responding appropriately to the speaker with nods, smiles, and clarifying questions; shutting out distracting thoughts, much like in meditation; focusing on what the speaker is saying; trying not to one-up the speaker by telling a similar or more impressive story; setting aside distracting items, such as a cell phone; and waiting to respond until the speaker is completely finished.

# Answers to Chapter 7: Comprehension Questions

1. *What stakeholder groups must you inform or educate when implementing mindfulness in a classroom or school?*

   The most important stakeholder groups to educate are classroom teachers, school leaders, parents, and students.

2. *What are the main action steps for a teacher implementing mindfulness in his or her classroom?*

   Typically, the first step is to learn about and practice mindfulness oneself. Then, the teacher should write a statement of intention, set specific goals, and plan how to reach them. He or she should also plan to monitor progress. The teacher should then communicate with school leaders and inform parents. Finally, mindfulness can be introduced to students.

3. *What are the benefits to schoolwide mindfulness programs?*

   When mindfulness is practiced across the school, there are shared goals among staff and students. Teachers give students tools to learn and practice mindfulness in all settings. They also hear common terms and vocabulary from many adults, leading them to internalize the concepts more quickly. Overall, schoolwide programs create consistency. In addition, schoolwide programs help educators because they can share resources and information with their colleagues.

4. *Why should teachers and students be allowed to opt out?*

   People should engage in mindfulness because they perceive its benefits, not because they have been forced to. Forcing people to practice mindfulness who dislike or are uninterested in it will create resentment instead of buy-in. Mindfulness is more effective when people practice it voluntarily.

# APPENDIX B

# NOTEWORTHY BOOKS, PROGRAMS, AND RESOURCES

Here you will find a list of notable books, magazines, programs, and other resources to help achieve mindfulness in the classroom.

## Books and Magazines

*Best Practices for Yoga in Schools* by Traci Childress and Jennifer Cohen Harper (2015)

Experienced yoga teachers and researchers wrote this helpful resource. It offers best practices for safe yoga and appeals to students of all ages. It includes specific how-to steps for creating yoga programming in schools.

*Blueberry Girl* by Neil Gaiman (2011), illustrated by Charles Vess

This book is appropriate for all ages. Originally written to celebrate the birth of a close friend's daughter, *Blueberry Girl* is an encouraging, inspirational book about hopes for the girl's life. Accompanying the text are beautiful illustrations of the wonders of the world.

*Child's Mind: Mindfulness Practices to Help Our Children Be More Focused, Calm, and Relaxed* by Christopher Willard (2010)

With helpful methods for teaching meditation and mindfulness practice to children and teenagers, this book is a great read for parents, educators, and others who work with youth. It is rife with practical definitions and metaphors, as well as doable activities.

*Everybody Present: Mindfulness in Education* by Nikolaj Flor Rotne and Didde Flor Rotne (2009)

This book, ideal for educators and school leaders, makes the case for mindfulness as a social change that must occur. It offers a clear description of mindfulness, along with ideas for teaching mindfulness to students and for strengthening one's own practice.

*A Handful of Quiet: Happiness in Four Pebbles* by Thich Nhat Hanh (2012)

This book uses the visual of four pebbles to teach meditation activities. Ideal for children or adolescents, it also encourages readers to see positive qualities in themselves.

*I Think, I Am! Teaching Kids the Power of Affirmations* by Louise L. Hay and Kristina Tracy (2008), illustrated by Manuela Schwarz

This book is appropriate for students in preschool through second grade. The authors teach children that the thoughts they think can have a big impact on their lives. It offers ways to change negative thoughts into powerful, positive affirmations.

*Managing the Inner World of Teaching* by Robert J. Marzano and Jana S. Marzano (2015)

This insightful book, written for those in education, offers a three-part model of understanding the inner world of emotions. These include developing a keen awareness of the following:

1. Emotional responses

2. Interpretations

3. Actions

The authors explain that developing an understanding of the interplay of emotional processes helps people have greater control over them.

*Mindful*, published by Shambhala Sun

This bimonthly magazine is rife with pertinent articles related to mindful living. With digital and print versions available, it is a wonderful resource for staying up to date with mindfulness topics such as how to meditate, quiet an anxious mind, and stay healthy.

*The Mindful Child: How to Help Your Kid Manage Stress and Become Happier, Kinder, and More Compassionate* by Susan Kaiser Greenland (2010)

This book details mindfulness activities appropriate for students in preschool through high school. The techniques help students develop social and emotional skills, as well as reduce their stress. In addition, the importance of mindfulness training is highlighted.

*Mindful Monkey, Happy Panda* by Lauren Alderfer (2011)

This book is appropriate for students of all ages. It opens with Monkey wondering why his friend Panda is so happy and peaceful all of the time. Monkey quickly learns that he has been suffering from "monkey mind," which means his mind is always filled with busy chatter. The book teaches the concept of attention and presence through these two adorable characters.

*Mindful Teaching and Teaching Mindfulness: A Guide for Anyone Who Teaches Anything* by Deborah Schoeberlein David (2009)

The author shares what it is like to be both a mindful educator and one who teaches mindfulness to students. She promotes an educational atmosphere filled with compassion, empathy, warmth, gratitude, and awareness both inside and outside the classroom.

*Peaceful Piggy Meditation* by Kerry Lee MacLean (2004)

Ideal for preschool through third grade, this delightful story features young pigs who use meditation to bring a sense of peace to their stressful and very busy, noisy lives. MacLean, a meditation therapist for children, concludes the tale by providing age-appropriate meditation techniques.

*The Secret of Saying Thanks* by Douglas Wood (2005), illustrated by Greg Shed

This book is ideal for students in kindergarten through third grade. It offers fresh insight into what it means to have a grateful heart. Students learn to be grateful for sunshine as it welcomes a new day.

*Unbeatable Mind: Forge Resiliency and Mental Toughness to Succeed at an Elite Level* by Mark Divine (2014)

Written by a former Navy SEAL, this book appeals to high school students and student athletes, as well as educators and coaches. Divine offers several techniques for self-mastery, including box breathing. He also shares strategies for developing emotional resilience and mental fortitude.

## Programs

### Calm Classroom (www.calmclassroom.com)

This site offers research-based schoolwide programming for various grade bands: high school, middle school, elementary school, and preschool. It offers strategies that take very little time to conduct but have a great impact on students' self-awareness, attention, and serenity.

### Mindful Schools (www.mindfulschools.org)

This website offers online training for educators who are interested in using mindfulness techniques in the classroom. Various courses are available, from an introductory mindfulness course to a yearlong certification course for those wanting to deepen their practice.

### Mindful Teachers (www.mindfulteachers.org)

This helpful site, written by Catharine Hannay, a teacher of adult English for speakers of other languages, offers free activities to educators for teaching students mindfulness, gratitude, compassion, and social and emotional skills, as well as helpful posts and links to resources on mindfulness. It also includes resources and links for teacher self-care. In addition, Hannay posts interviews with teachers who have taught mindfulness to people of all ages.

### MindUP (www.thehawnfoundation.org/mindup)

MindUP is a social and emotional literacy program. Founder Goldie Hawn worked with cognitive psychologists and neuroscientists to develop fifteen-lesson curricula that are appropriately designed to meet the unique needs of various age groups: K–2, 3–5, and 6–8. Students learn to self-regulate their behavior and focus their attention. The results of the program are promising, reporting improved self-concept and optimism, increased academic achievement, and better social relationships.

### Move with Me Yoga Adventures (www.move-with-me.com)

This site offers information, resources, training, and curriculum materials related to mindfulness for elementary school children. The programming primarily focuses on developing self-regulation skills through yoga and other movement activities.

## Resources

### Collaborative for Academic, Social, and Emotional Learning (www.casel.org)

The Collaborative for Academic, Social, and Emotional Learning (CASEL) is a nonprofit organization whose mission is to promote the inclusion of social-emotional learning in the K–12 curriculum. CASEL has a team of researchers whose work can provide guidance and support to schools in the areas of social and emotional learning. The CASEL website offers a library of research and resources. In addition to conducting research, CASEL has worked to help influence policy makers to acknowledge the benefits of social and emotional learning.

**The Free Mindfulness Project** (www.freemindfulness.org)

Established by Peter Morgan, a clinical psychologist and mindfulness teacher, The Free Mindfulness Project offers resources that can be freely used and distributed. From definitions of mindfulness to mindfulness apps to poetry, this site offers easy access to a myriad of resources that may be beneficial to the teacher as a mindfulness practitioner and as an educator in the classroom.

**Mindful** (www.mindful.org)

Mindful, the website associated with the magazine of the same name, is a free resource offering personal stories, insights, advice, videos, and inspiration to those who want to live mindfully. Readers can learn about effective techniques, practical advice, as well as the science of mindfulness in short, easy-to-read segments. Although not written specifically for schools, this site is immensely helpful for novice and veteran practitioners of mindfulness.

**Mindfulness for Students** (www.mindfulnessforstudents.co.uk)

This website offers free resources for students and staff wanting to practice mindfulness. It includes an explanation of the why of mindfulness, mindfulness activities, free guided meditations, and a list of helpful resources. The site also includes resources specific to educators.

**Still Quiet Place** (www.stillquietplace.com)

On this comprehensive website, Amy Saltzman provides numerous mindfulness resources for classroom educators including a blog, recommended books, links to training sites, and much more.

# REFERENCES

Adams, C. (2011). Recess makes kids smarter. *Scholastic Teacher*. Accessed at www.scholastic.com /teachers/article/recess-makes-kids-smarter on July 28, 2016.

Alderfer, L. (2011). *Mindful monkey, happy panda*. Somerville, MA: Wisdom Publications.

American Academy of Pediatrics. (2014). *Helping children handle stress*. Accessed at www.healthychildren .org/English/healthy-living/emotional-wellness/Pages/Helping-Children-Handle-Stress.aspx on July 28, 2016.

American Psychological Association. (2009). *Stress in America*. Accessed at www.apa.org/news/press /releases/stress/2009/stress-exec-summary.pdf on July 28, 2016.

American Psychological Association. (2014). *American psychology survey shows teen stress rivals that of adults* [Press release]. Accessed at www.apa.org/news/press/releases/2014/02/teen-stress.aspx on July 28, 2016.

Arch, J. J., & Craske, M. G. (2006). Mechanisms of mindfulness: Emotion regulation following a focused breathing induction. *Behavior Research and Therapy, 44*, 1849–1858.

*Attention.* (n.d.). Accessed at www.psychologytoday.com/basics/attention on July 28, 2016.

Baer, D. (2014, August 5). Search inside yourself: Google's life changing mindfulness course. *Business Insider*. Accessed at www.businessinsider.com/search-inside-yourself-googles-life-changing -mindfulness-course-2014-8 on July 28, 2016.

Baer, R. A. (2014). *Mindfulness-based treatment approaches* (2nd ed.). San Diego, CA: Academic Press.

Baer, R. A., Smith, G. T., Hopkins, J., Krietemeyer, J., & Toney, L. (2006). Using self-report assess-ment methods to explore facets of mindfulness. *Assessment, 13*, 27–45.

Bandura, A. (1994). Self-efficacy. In V. S. Ramachaudran (Ed.), *Encyclopedia of human behavior* (Vol. 4, pp. 71–81). New York: Academic Press. (Reprinted in *Encyclopedia of mental health*, by H. Friedman, Ed., 1998, San Diego: Academic Press)

Barth, P. (2008). Time out: Is recess in danger? *Center for Public Education*. Accessed at www .centerforpubliceducation.org/Main-Menu/Organizing-a-school/Time-out-Is-recess-in-danger on July 28, 2016.

Bauerlein, M. (2011). Too dumb for complex texts? *Educational Leadership*, *68*(5), 28–32.

Beauchemin, J., Hutchins, T. L., & Patterson, F. (2008). Mindfulness meditation may lessen anxiety, promote social skills, and improve academic performance among adolescents with learning disabilities. *Journal of Evidence-Based Complementary & Alternative Medicine*, *13*(1), 34–45.

Begley, S. (2007). *Train your mind, change your brain: How a new science reveals our extraordinary potential to transform ourselves.* New York: Ballantine Books.

Benson, H. (2010). *The relaxation revolution: Enhancing your personal health through the science and genetics of mind body healing.* New York: Simon & Schuster.

Bernard, B. (2004). *Resiliency: What we have learned.* San Francisco: WestEd.

Bharati, S. J. (n.d.). *Four paths of yoga: Jnana, bhakti, karma, raja.* Accessed at www.swamij.com/four-paths-of-yoga.htm on July 28, 2016.

Biegel, G. M., Brown, K. W., Shapiro, S. L., & Schubert, C. M. (2009). Mindfulness-based stress reduction for the treatment of psychiatric outpatients: A randomized clinical trial. *Journal of Consulting and Clinical Psychology*, *77*(5), 855–866.

Black, D. S., & Fernando, R. (2014). Mindfulness training and classroom behavior among lower income and ethnic minority elementary school children. *Journal of Child and Family Studies*, *23*(7), 1242–1246.

Black, D. S., Milam, J., & Sussman, S. (2009, September). Sitting-meditation interventions among youth: A review of treatment efficacy. *Pediatrics*, *124*(3), 532–541.

Bohrnstedt, G. (2013). Gains and gaps: Education performance after *A Nation at Risk. American Institutes for Research.* Accessed at www.air.org/resource/three-decades-education-reform-are-we-still-nation-risk#Bohrnstedt on July 28, 2016.

Boyatzis, R. E. (1982). *The competent manager: A model for effective performance.* New York: Wiley.

Brackett, M. A., & Simmons, D. (2015). Emotions matter: Cultivating the emotional intelligence of both students and teachers is our best hope for safe, caring, and effective schools. *Educational Leadership*, *73*(2), 22–27.

Bridgeland, J., Bruce, M., & Hariharan, A. (2013). *The missing piece: A national teacher survey on how social and emotional learning can empower children and transform schools* [Research report]. Accessed at www.casel.org/library/the-missing-piece on July 28, 2016.

Broderick, P. C., & Metz, S. (2009). Learning to BREATHE: A pilot trial of mindfulness curriculum for adolescents. *Advances in School Mental Health Promotion*, *2*(1), 35–46.

Brown, K. W., Creswell, J. D., & Ryan, R. M. (Eds.). (2015). *Handbook of mindfulness: Theory, research, and practice.* New York: Guilford Press.

Buckley, A. (2003). *The kids' yoga deck: 50 poses and games.* San Francisco: Chronicle Books.

Bushaw, W. J., & Lopez, S. J. (2010, September). A time for change: The 42nd annual Phi Delta Kappa/Gallup poll of the public's attitudes toward the public schools. *Kappan Magazine*, *92*(1), 9–26.

Cahn, B. R., & Polich, J. (2006). Meditation states and traits: EEG, ERP, and neuroimaging studies. *Psychological Bulletin, 132*, 180–211. doi:10.1037/0033–2909.132.2.180

Canfield, J. (1990). Improving students' self-esteem: Using a 10-step system, teachers can help strengthen their students' self-esteem and increase their chances for success in life. *Educational Leadership, 48*(1), 48–50.

Carmody, J., & Baer, R. A. (2008). Relationships between mindfulness practice and levels of mindfulness, medical and psychological symptoms, and well-being in a mindfulness based stress reduction program. *Journal of Behavioral Medicine, 31*(1), 23–33.

Center on Education Policy. (2007). *Choices, changes, and challenges: Curriculum and instruction in the NCLB era*. Washington, DC: Author.

Centers for Disease Control and Prevention. (2013). Youth risk behavior surveillance—United States 2013. *Surveillance Summaries, 63*(4).

Chambers, R., Lo, B. C. Y., & Allen, N. B. (2008). The impact of intensive mindfulness training on attentional control, cognitive style, and affect. *Cognitive Therapy and Research, 32*, 303–322.

Chetty, R., Friedman, J. N., & Rockoff, J. E. (2011). *The long-term impacts of teachers: Teacher value-added and student outcomes in adulthood* [NBER Working Paper No. 17699]. Cambridge, MA: National Bureau of Economic Research.

Childress, T. M., & Harper, J. C. (Eds.). (2015). *Best practices for yoga in schools* (Yoga Service Best Practices Guide Vol. 1). Atlanta, GA: YSC-Omega Publications.

Chou, H. T., & Edge, N. (2012). "They are happier and having better lives than I am": The impact of using Facebook on perceptions of others' lives. *Cyberpsychology, Behavior, and Social Networking, 15*(2), 117–121. doi: 10.1089/cyber.2011.0324

Christakis, D. (2011). *Media and children* [Video file]. Accessed at www.youtube.com/watch?v=BoT7qH_uVNo on October 28, 2016.

Corcoran, K. M., Farb, N., Anderson, A., & Segal, Z. V. (2010). Mindfulness and emotional regulation: Outcomes and possible mediating mechanisms. In A. M. Kring & D. M. Sloan (Eds.), *Emotion regulation and psychopathology: A transdiagnostic approach to etiology and treatment* (pp. 339–355). New York: Guilford Press.

Csikszentmihalyi, M. (1990). *Flow: The psychology of an optimal experience*. New York: HarperCollins.

Cuddy, A. (2015). *Presence: Bring your boldest self to your biggest challenges*. New York: Little, Brown.

Dahl, J., Wilson, K. G., & Nilsson, A. (2004). Acceptance and commitment therapy and the treatment of persons at risk for long-term disability resulting from stress and pain symptoms: A preliminary randomized trial. *Behavior Therapy, 35*, 785–802.

Dalrymple, K. L., & Herbert, J. D. (2007). Acceptance and commitment therapy for generalized social anxiety disorder: A pilot study. *Behavior Modification, 31*(5), 543–568. doi: 10.1177/0145445507302037

David, D. S. (2009). *Mindful teaching and teaching mindfulness: A guide for anyone who teaches anything*. Somerville, MA: Wisdom.

Davidson, R., Dunne, J., Eccles, J., Engle, A., Greenberg, M., Jennings, P., et al. (2012). Contemplative practice and mental training: Prospects for American education. *Child Development Perspectives, 6,* 146–153.

Davidson, R. J., Kabat-Zinn, J., Schumacher, J., Rosenkranz, M., Muller, D., Santorelli, S. F., et al. (2003). Alterations in brain and immune function produced by mindfulness meditation. *Psychosomatic Medicine, 65*(4), 564–570.

Davis, M. (2016, May 6). Resources for parents, teachers, and administrators. *Edutopia.* Accessed at www.edutopia.org/blogs/tag/career-technical-education on October 28, 2016.

Diamond, M., & Hopson, J. (1998). *Magic trees of the mind: How to nurture your child's intelligence, creativity, and healthy emotions from birth through adolescence.* New York: Penguin.

Divine, M. (2014). *Unbeatable mind: Forge resiliency and mental toughness to succeed at an elite level.* Encinitas, CA: Author.

Dyer, W. (2004). *The power of intention.* New York: Hay House.

Elias, M. J., Zins, J. E., Weissberg, R. P., Frey, K. S., Greenberg, M. T., Haynes, N. M., et al. (1997). *Promoting social and emotional learning: Guidelines for educators.* Alexandria, VA: Association for Supervision and Curriculum Development.

Emmons, R. (2010). *Thanks! How the new science of gratitude can make you happier.* Boston: Houghton-Mifflin Harcourt.

Every Student Succeeds Act of 2015, Pub. L. No. 114-95 § 114 Stat. 1177 (2015).

Flook, L., & Fuligni, A. J. (2008). Family and school spillover in adolescents' daily lives. *Child Development, 79,* 776–787.

Flook, L., & Smalley, S. L. (2010). Effects of mindfulness awareness practices on executive functions in elementary school children. *Journal of Applied Psychology, 26,* 70–95.

Flor Rotne, N., & Flor Rotne, D. (2009). *Everybody present: Mindfulness in education.* Berkeley, CA: Parallax Press.

Franklin, D. (2012). How hospital gardens help patients heal. *Scientific American.* Accessed at www.scientificamerican.com/article/nature-that-nurtures on October 28, 2016.

Gaiman, N. (2011). *Blueberry girl.* New York: HarperCollins Children's.

Gazella, K. (2005). Bringing mindfulness to medicine: An interview with Jon Kabat-Zinn. *Advances in Mind-Body Medicine, 21*(2), 23.

Glasser, W. (1998). *Choice theory: A new psychology of personal freedom.* New York: HarperCollins.

Glasser, W. (2006). *Every student can succeed: Finally a book that explains how to reach and teach every student in your school.* San Diego, CA: Black Forest Book Promotions.

Goldin, P. R., & Gross, J. J. (2010). Effects of mindfulness-based stress reduction (MBSR) on emotion regulation in social anxiety disorder. *Emotion, 10,* 83–91. doi:10.1037/a0018441

Goldstein, E. D. (2007). Sacred moments: Implications on well-being and stress. *Journal of Clinical Psychology, 63,* 1001–1019.

Goleman, D. (1995). *Emotional intelligence.* New York: Bantam Books.

Goleman, D. (1998). *Working with emotional intelligence.* New York: Bantam Books.

Goleman, D. (2013) *Focus: The hidden driver of excellence.* New York: HarperCollins.

Greenland, S. K. (2010). *The mindful child: How to help your kid manage stress and become happier, kinder, and more compassionate.* New York: Atria Books.

Gregory, G., & Kaufeldt, M. (2015). *The motivated brain: Improving student attention, engagement, and perseverance.* Alexandria, VA: Association for Supervision and Curriculum Development.

Grinde, B., & Patil, G. G. (2009). Biophilia: Does visual contact with nature impact on health and well-being? *International Journal of Environment Research and Public Health.* Accessed at www.mdpi.com/1660-4601/6/9/2332/htm on July 28, 2016.

Grossman, P., Niemann, L., Schmidt, S., & Walach, H. (2004). Mindfulness-based stress reduction and health benefits: A meta-analysis. *Journal of Psychosomatic Research, 57*(1), 35–43.

Haidt, J. (2006). *The happiness hypothesis: Finding modern truth in ancient wisdom.* New York: Basic Books.

Haier, R. J., Jung, R. E., Yeo, R. A., Head, K., & Alkire, M. T. (2004). Structural brain variations and general intelligence. *Neuroimage, 23,* 425–433.

Hale, J. A. (1998). *Healing art: Young children coping with stress.* Birmingham, AL: Alabama Association for Young Children.

Hampton, K. N., Goulet, L. S., Marlow, C., & Rainie, L. (2012). *Why most Facebook users get more than they give: The effect of Facebook 'power users' on everybody else.* Accessed at http://pewinternet.org/Reports/2012/Facebook-users.aspx on February 10, 2013.

Hanson, R. (2009). *Buddha's brain: The practical neuroscience of happiness, love & wisdom.* Oakland, CA: New Harbinger Publications.

Harris, R. (2006, August). Embracing your demons: An overview of acceptance and commitment therapy. *Psychotherapy in Australia, 12,* 4.

Hattie, J. (1992). Measuring the effects of schooling. *Australian Journal of Education, 36*(1), 5–13.

Hattie, J. (2009). *Visible learning: A synthesis of over 800 meta-analyses relating to achievement.* New York: Routledge.

Hattie, J. (2012). *Visible learning for teachers: Amazing impact on learning.* New York: Routledge.

Hay, L. L., & Tracy, K. (2008). *I think I am: Teaching kids the power of affirmations.* New York: Hay House.

Hendrick, B. (2010). *Internet overuse may cause depression.* Accessed at www.webmd.com/depression/news/20100802/internet-overuse-may-cause-depression on July 28, 2016.

Hoffman, S. G., Sawyer, A. T., Witt, A. A., & Oh, D. (2010). The effect of mindfulness-based therapy on anxiety and depression: A meta-analytic review. *Journal of Consulting and Clinical Psychology, 78,* 169–183.

Hölzel, B. K., Ott, U., Gard, T., Hempel, H., Weygandt, M., Morgan, K., et al. (2008). Investigation of mindfulness meditation practitioners with voxel-base morphometry. *Social Cognitive and Affective Neuroscience, 3*, 55–61.

Hughlett, M. (2013, November 24). Mindfulness arrives in the workplace. *Star Tribune.* Accessed at www.startribune.com/mindfulness-arrives-in-the-twin-cities workplace/233176121/ on July 28, 2016.

Jensen, E. (2005). *Teaching with the brain in mind.* Alexandria, VA: Association for Supervision and Curriculum Development.

Jha, A. P., Stanley, E. A., Kiyonaga, A., Wong, L., & Gelfand, L. (2010). Examining the protective effects of mindfulness on working memory capacity and affective experience. *Emotion, 10*(1), 54–64.

Johnson, D., Thom, N. J., Stanley, E. D., Haase, L., Simmons, A. N., Pei-An, S., et al. (2014). Modifying resilience mechanisms in at-risk individuals: A controlled study of mindfulness training in marines preparing for deployment. *American Journal of Psychiatry, 171*(8), 844–853.

Kabat-Zinn, J. (1994). *Wherever you go there you are: Mindfulness meditation in everyday life.* New York: Hyperion.

Kabat-Zinn, J. (1996). Mindfulness meditation: What it is, what it isn't, and its role in health care and medicine. In Y. Haruki, Y. Ishii, & M. Suzuki (Eds.), *Comparative and psychological study on meditation* (pp. 161–169). Delft, the Netherlands: Eburon.

Kabat-Zinn, J. (2005). *Coming to our senses: Healing ourselves and the world through mindfulness.* New York: Hyperion.

Kandel, E. (2006). *In search of memory: The emergence of a new science of mind.* New York: Norton.

Kemeny, M. E., Foltz, C., Cavanagh, J. F., Cullen, M., Giese-Davis, J., Jennings, P., et al. (2012). Contemplative/emotion training reduces negative emotional behavior and promotes prosocial responses. *Emotion, 12*(2), 338–350.

Keng, S., Smoski, M. J., & Robins, C. J. (2011). Effects of mindfulness on psychological health: A review of empirical studies. *Clinical Psychology Review, 31*, 1041–1056.

Kerr, C. E., Jones, S. R., Wan, Q., Pritchett, D. L., Wasserman, R. H., Wexler, A., et al. (2011). Effects of mindfulness meditation training on anticipatory alpha mood in primary somatosensory cortex. *Brain Research Bulletin, 85*, 96–103.

KidsHealth. (2016). *Yoga.* Accessed at http://kidshealth.org/en/teens/yoga.html on July 28, 2016.

Kocovski, N. L., Fleming, J. E., & Rector, N. A. (2009). Mindfulness and acceptance-based group therapy for social anxiety disorder: An open trial. *Cognitive and Behavioral Practice, 16*(3), 276–289. doi: 10.1016/j.cbpra.2008.12.004

Koszycki, D., Benger, M., Shlik, J., & Bradwejn, J. (2007). Randomized trial of a meditation based stress reduction program and cognitive behavior therapy in generalized social anxiety disorder. *Behaviour Research and Therapy, 45*(10), 2518–2526. doi: 10.1016/j.brat.2007.04.011

Kross, E., Verduyn, P., Demiralp, E., Park, J., Lee, D. S., Lin, N., et al. (2013). Facebook use predicts declines in subjective well-being in young adults. *PLOS ONE.* doi: 10.1371/journal.pone.0069841

Kuhlman, S., Kirschbaum, C., & Wolf, O. T. (2005). Effects of oral cortisol treatment in healthy young women on memory retrieval of negative and neutral words. *Neurobiology of Learning and Memory, 83,* 158–162.

Kuo, F. E., & Sullivan, W. C. (2001). Environment and crime in the inner city: Does vegetation reduce crime? *Environment and Behavior, 33*(3), 343–367.

Langer, E. (2014). *Mindfulness* (25th anniversary ed.). Boston: Da Capo Press.

Lazarus, R. S., & Folkman, S. (1984). *Stress, appraisal, and coping.* New York: Springer.

Lewis, M. D. (2005). Self-organizing individual difference in brain development. *Developmental Review, 25,* 252–277.

Linden, W. (1973). Practicing of meditation by school children and their levels of field dependence-independence, test anxiety, and reading achievement. *Journal of Consulting and Clinical Psychology, 41*(1), 139–143.

Linehan, M. (1993). *Cognitive-behavioral treatment of borderline personality disorder.* New York: Guilford Press.

Luders, E., Toga, A. W., Lepore, N., & Gaser, C. (2009). The underlying anatomical correlates of long-term meditation: Larger hippocampal and frontal volumes of gray matter. *Neuroimage, 45,* 672–678.

Lutz, A., Slagter, A., Dunne, J. D., & Davidson, R. J. (2008). Attention regulation and monitoring in meditation. *Trends in Cognitive Sciences, 12,* 163–169.

Lyubomirsky, S. (2008). *The how of happiness: A scientific approach for getting the life you want.* New York: Penguin Press.

MacLean, K. A., Ferrer, E., Aichele, S. R., Bridwell, D. A., Zanesco, A. P., Jacobs, T. L., et al. (2010). Intensive meditation training improves perceptual discrimination and sustained attention. *Psychological Science, 21*(6), 829–839.

MacLean, K. L. (2004). *Peaceful piggy meditation.* Park Ridge, IL: Albert Whitman Prairie Books.

Malinowski, P. (2013). Neural mechanisms of attentional control in mindfulness meditation. *Frontiers in Neuroscience.* doi: 10.3389/fnins.2013.00008

Marzano, R. J. (with Marzano, J. S., & Pickering, D. J.). (2003). *Classroom management that works: Research-based strategies for every teacher.* Alexandria, VA: Association for Supervision and Curriculum Development.

Marzano, R. J. (2007). *The art and science of teaching: A comprehensive framework for effective instruction.* Alexandria, VA: Association for Supervision and Curriculum Development.

Marzano, R. J. (2012). *Becoming a reflective teacher.* Bloomington, IN: Marzano Research.

Marzano, R. J., Frontier, T., & Livingston, D. (2011). *Effective supervision: Supporting the art and science of teaching.* Alexandria, VA: Association for Supervision and Curriculum Development.

Marzano, R. J., & Marzano, J. S. (2015). *Managing the inner world of teaching: Emotions, interpretations, and actions.* Bloomington, IN: Marzano Research.

Marzano, R. J., Pickering, D. J., & Pollock, J. E. (2001). *Classroom instruction that works: Research-based strategies for increasing student achievement.* Alexandria, VA: Association for Supervision and Curriculum Development.

Marzano, R., Scott, D., Boogren, T. H., & Newcomb, M. L. (2017). *Motivating and inspiring students: Strategies to awaken the learner.* Bloomington, IN: Marzano Research.

Maslow, A. H. (1943). A theory of human motivation. *Psychological Review, 50*(4), 370–396.

Maslow, A. H. (1969). The farther reaches of human nature. *Journal of Transpersonal Psychology, 1*(1), 1–9.

Mayo Clinic. (2014). *Stress management.* Accessed at www.mayoclinic.org/tests-procedures/stress-management/basics/definition/prc-20021046 on July 29, 2016.

Mayo Clinic. (2016). *Chronic stress puts your health at risk.* Accessed at www.mayoclinic.org/healthy-lifestyle/stress-management/in-depth/stress/art-20046037 on July 29, 2016.

McGonigal, J. (2015). *Superbetter: A revolutionary approach to getting stronger, happier, braver and more resilient—powered by the science of games.* New York: Penguin Books.

McKim, R. D. (2008). Rumination as a mediator of the effects of mindfulness: Mindfulness based stress reduction (MBSR) with a heterogeneous community sample experiencing anxiety, depression, and/or chronic pain. *Dissertation Abstracts International: Section B: The Sciences and Engineering, 68,* 7673.

McTigue, E. M., & Rimm-Kaufman, S. E. (2011). The responsive classroom approach and its implications for improving reading and writing. *Reading & Writing Quarterly: Overcoming Learning Difficulties, 27,* 5–24.

Medina, J. (2014). *Brain rules: 12 principles for surviving and thriving at work, home, and school* (Updated and expanded ed.). Seattle, WA: Pear Press.

Meiklejohn, J., Phillips, C., Freedman, M. L., Griffin, M. L., Biegel, G., Roach, A., et al. (2012). Integrating mindfulness training into K–12 education: Fostering the resilience of teachers and students. *Mindfulness, 3*(4), 291–307. doi: 10.1007/s12671-012-0094-5

MetLife. (2002). *The MetLife survey of the American teacher 2002—Student life: School, home, and community.* New York: Author.

Monk, C. A., Trafton, J. G, & Boehm-Davis, D. A. (2008). The effect of interruption duration and demand on resuming suspended goals. *Journal of Experimental Psychology: Applied, 14*(4), 299–313.

Moore, A., & Malinowski, P. (2009). Meditation, mindfulness and cognitive flexibility. *Consciousness and Cognition, 18,* 176–186.

Mrazek, M., Franklin, M., Tarchin-Phillips, D., Baird, B., & Schooler, J. (2013). Mindfulness training improves working memory capacity and GRE performance while reducing mind wandering. *Psychological Science, 24*(5), 776–781.

Mukpo, D., & Gimian, C. (2006). *Dragon thunder: My life with Chogyam Trungpa.* Boston: Shambhala.

Myint, K., Choy, K. L., Su, T. T., & Lam, S. K. (2011). The effect of short-term practice of mindfulness meditation in alleviating stress in university students. *Biomedical Research, 22*(2), 165–171.

Napoli, M., Krech, P. R., & Holley, L. C. (2005). Mindfulness training for elementary school students: The attention academy. *Journal of Applied School Psychology, 21*, 99–125.

National Academies Institute of Medicine. (2013, May 23). *Schools should provide opportunities for 60 minutes of daily physical activity for all students.* Accessed at www8.nationalacademies.org/onpinews /newsitem.aspx?RecordID=18314 on October 28, 2016.

National Center for Education Statistics. (2012). *Selected findings from PISA 2012.* Accessed at http:// nces.ed.gov/survey/pisa/pisa2012highlights_1.asp on July 28, 2016.

National Commission on Excellence in Education. (1983). *A nation at risk: The imperative for school reform.* Accessed at www2.ed.gov/pubs/NatAtRisk/index.html on July 29, 2016.

Neff, K. (2011). *Self-compassion: The proven power of being kind to yourself.* New York: HarperCollins.

Neporent, L. (2014, January 30). Seattle Seahawks will have the 'ohm' team advantage. *ABC News.* Accessed at http://abcnews.go.com/Health/seattle-seahawks-ohm-team-advantage/story?id=21614481 on July 28, 2016.

Nhat Hanh, T. (2012). *A handful of quiet: Happiness in four pebbles.* Berkeley, CA: Plum Blossom Books.

Nhat Hanh, T. (2015). *Silence: The power of quiet in a world full of noise.* New York: HarperCollins.

No Child Left Behind (NCLB) Act of 2001, Pub. L. No. 107-110, § 115, Stat. 1425 (2002).

Noggle, J. J., Steiner, N. J., Minami, T., & Khalsa, S. B. (2012). Benefits of yoga for psychological well-being in a US high school curriculum: A preliminary randomized control trial. *Journal of Developmental & Behavioral Pediatrics, 33*(3), 193–201.

Novotney, A. (2011). Silence, please: Psychologists are increasing awareness of the harmful effects noise has on cognition and health. *Monitor on Psychology, 42*(7), 46.

O'Neill, J., & Conzemius, A. (2006). *The power of SMART goals: Using goals to improve student learning.* Bloomington, IN: Solution Tree Press.

Ortner, C. N. M., Kilner, S. J., & Zelazo, P. D. (2007). Mindfulness meditation and reduced emotional interference on a cognitive task. *Motivation and Emotion, 31*, 271–283. doi: 10.1007 /s11031-007–9076-7

Pagnoni, G., & Cekic, M. (2007). Age effects on gray matter volume and attentional performance in Zen meditation. *Neurobiology of Aging, 28*(10), 1623–1627.

Panksepp, J., & Biven, L. (2012). *The archaeology of mind: Neuroevolutionary origins of human emotion.* New York: Norton.

Pasricha, N. (2016). *The happiness equation: Want nothing + do anything = have everything.* New York: G. P. Putnam's Sons.

Payton, J., Weissberg, R. P., Durlak, J. A., Dymnicki, A. B., Taylor, R. D., Schellinger, K. B., et al. (2008). *The positive impact of social and emotional learning for kindergarten to eighth-grade students: Findings from three scientific reviews.* Chicago: Collaborative for Academic, Social, and Emotional Learning.

Pepping, C. A., O'Donovan, A., & Davis, P. J. (2013). The positive effects of mindfulness on self-esteem. *The Journal of Positive Psychology, 8*(5), 376–386.

Phelan, J. P. (2010). Mindfulness as presence. *Mindfulness, 1*(2), 131–134.

Posner, M. I., & Rothbart, M. K. (1992). Attention and conscious experience. In A. D. Milner & M. D. Rugg (Eds.), *The neuropsychology of consciousness* (pp. 91–112). London: Academic Press.

Public Agenda. (1994). *First things first: What Americans expect from the public schools.* New York: Author.

Public Agenda. (1997). *Getting by: What American teenagers really think about their schools.* New York: Author.

Public Agenda. (2002). *A lot easier said than done: Parents talk about raising children in today's America.* New York: Author.

Rajamaki, S. (2011). *Mindfulness-based stress reduction: Does mindfulness training affect competence based self-esteem and burnout?* (Master's dissertation, Stockholm University, Sweden). Accessed at http://su.diva-portal.org/smash/get/diva2:423222/FULLTEXT101 on July 28, 2016.

Ramel, W., Goldin, P. R., Carmona, P. E., & McQuaid, J. R. (2004). The effects of mindfulness meditation on cognitive processes and affect in patients with past depression. *Cognitive Therapy and Research, 28,* 433–455.

Rani, N. J., & Rao, P. V. (1996). Meditation and attention regulation. *Journal of Indian Psychology, 14,* 26–30.

Rasmussen, M. K., & Pidgeon, A. M. (2011). The direct and indirect benefits of dispositional mindfulness on self-esteem and social anxiety. *Anxiety, Stress, & Coping, 24,* 227–233.

Ratey, J. J. (2008). *Spark: The revolutionary new science of exercise and the brain.* New York: Little, Brown.

Rechtschaffen, D., & Rechtschaffen, T. (2015). The five literacies of mindful learning. *Educational Leadership, 73*(2), 58–62.

Rempel, K. D. (2012). Mindfulness for children and youth: A review of the literature with an argument for school-based implementation. *Canadian Journal of Counselling and Psychotherapy, 46*(3), 201–220.

Ricard, M. (2010). *Why meditate? Working with thoughts and emotions.* New York: Hay House.

Robertson, I. H., Manly, T., Andrade, J., Baddeley, B. T., & Yiend, J. (1997). 'Oops!': Performance correlates of everyday attentional failures in traumatic brain injured and normal subjects. *Neuropsychologia, 35*(6), 747–758.

Rozin, P., & Royzman, E. B. (2001). Negativity bias, negativity dominance, and contagion. *Personality and Psychology Review, 5*(4), 296–320.

Salovey, P., & Mayer, J. D. (1995). *The experiment on self-awareness and handling stress well.* Washington, DC: American Psychological Press.

Salovey, P., Mayer, J. D., Goldman, S. L., Turvey, C., & Palfai, T. P. (1995). Emotional attention, clarity, and repair: Exploring emotional intelligence using the Trait Meta-Mood Scale. In J. Pennebaker (Ed.), *Emotion, disclosure, and health* (pp. 125–154). Washington, DC: American Psychological Association.

Schmertz, S. K., Anderson, P. L., & Robins, D. L. (2009). The relationship between self-reported mindfulness and performance on tasks of sustained attention. *Journal of Psychopathy and Behavioral Assessment, 31*(1), 60–66.

Schonert-Reichl, K. A., & Lawlor, M. S. (2010). The effects of mindfulness-based program on pre- and early adolescents' well-being and social and emotional competence. *Mindfulness, 1*(3), 137–151.

Schonert-Reichl, K. A., Oberle, E., Lawlor, M. S., Abbott, D., & Thomson, A. (2015). Enhancing cognitive and social-emotional development through a simple-to-administer mindfulness-based school program for elementary school children: A randomized controlled trial. *Developmental Psychology, 51*(1), 52–66.

Scott, D., & Marzano, R. J. (2014). *Awaken the learner: Finding the source of effective education.* Bloomington, IN: Marzano Research.

Sebanc, A. M. (2003). The friendship features of preschool children: Links with prosocial behavior and aggression. *Social Development, 12*(2), 249–268.

Seligman, M. E. P. (2006). *Learned optimism: How to change your mind and your life.* New York: Vintage.

Semple, R. J., Lee, J., & Miller, L. F. (2006). Mindfulness-based cognitive therapy for children. In R. A. Baer (Ed.), *Mindfulness-based cognitive approaches: Clinician's guide to evidence base and applications.* Burlington, MA: Academic Press.

Shapiro, S. L., Astin, J. A., Bishop, S. R., & Cordova, M. (2005). Mindfulness-based stress reduction for health care professionals: Results from a randomized trial. *International Journal of Stress Management, 12*, 164–176.

Shapiro, S. L., Brown, K. W., & Biegel, G. M. (2007). Teaching self-care to caregivers: Effects of mindfulness-based stress reduction on the mental health of therapists in training. *Training and Education in Professional Psychology, 1*(2), 105–115.

Shattock, E. H. (1958). *An experiment in mindfulness: An English admiral's experiences in a Buddhist monastery.* New York: Dutton.

Siegel, D. J. (2007). *The mindful brain: Reflection and attunement in the cultivation of well-being.* New York: Norton.

Siegel, D. J. (2010). *The mindful therapist: A clinician's guide to mindsight and neural integration.* New York: Norton.

Siegel, R. D. (2013). *Positive psychology: Harnessing the power of happiness, personal strength, and mindfulness.* Boston: Harvard Health Publications.

Sousa, D. A. (2011). *How the brain learns* (4th ed.). Thousand Oaks, CA: Corwin Press.

Spiegler, M. D., & Guevremont, D. C. (2010). *Contemporary behavior therapy* (5th ed.). Belmont, CA: Wadsworth.

Stanley, E. A., Schaldach, J. M., Kiyonaga, A., & Jha, A. P. (2011). Mindfulness-based mind fitness training: A case study of high stress pre-deployment military cohort. *Cognitive and Behavioral Practice, 12,* 566–576.

Steinberg, L. (2014). *Age of opportunity: Lessons from the new science of adolescence.* New York: Houghton Mifflin Harcourt.

Stuhlman, M., & Pianta, R. (2009). Profiles of educational quality in first grade. *The Elementary School Journal, 109*(4), 323–342.

Suffield, J. S. (2012). *A role-play notebook: Questions that really make a difference!* (3rd ed.). Raleigh, NC: Lulu Press.

Sung, I. (2013). Data points to behavioral health as a growing challenge for pediatrics. *Athenahealth.* Accessed at www.athenahealth.com/blog/2013/10/28/data-points-to-behavioral-health-as-a -growing-challenge-for-pediatricians on July 28, 2016.

Tan, C.-M., Goleman, D., & Kabat-Zinn, J. (2012). *Search inside yourself: The unexpected path to achieving success, happiness (and world peace).* New York: HarperCollins.

Tang, Y. Y., Ma, Y., Wang, J., Fan, Y., Feng, S., Lu, Q., et al. (2007). Short-term meditation training improves attention and self-regulation. *Proceedings of the National Academy of Sciences, 104*(43), 17152–17156.

Teasdale, J. D. (1999). Metacognition, mindfulness and the modification of mood disorders. *Clinical Psychology and Psychotherapy, 6*(2), 146–155.

Thompson, B. L., & Waltz, J. A. (2008). Mindfulness, self-esteem, and unconditional self acceptance. *Journal of Rational Emotive Cognitive Behavior Therapy, 26,* 119–126.

Thompson, R. A. (1994). Emotion regulation: A theme in search of a definition. *Monographs of the Society for Research in Child Development, 59*(2/3), 25–52.

Tollenaar, M. S., Elzinga, B. M., Spinhoven, P., & Everaerd, W. (2009). Immediate and prolonged effects of cortisol, but not propranolol, on memory retrieval in healthy young men. *Neurobiology of Learning and Memory, 91,* 23–31.

Tomkinson, C. (1995). *Big sky mind: Buddhism and the beat generation.* New York: Riverhead Trade.

Tough, P. (2012). *How children succeed: Grit, curiosity, and the hidden power of character.* New York: Houghton Mifflin Harcourt.

Twohig, M. P., Hayes, S. C., & Masuda, A. (2006). Increasing willingness to experience obsessions: Acceptance and commitment therapy as a treatment for obsessive compulsive disorder. *Behavior Therapy, 37*(1), 3–13.

Ulrich, R. S. (1984). View through a window may influence recovery from surgery. *Science, 224*(4647), 420–421.

U.S. Department of Health and Human Services. (2001). *Trends in the well-being of America's children and youth, 2001.* Washington, DC: U.S. Government Printing Office.

Waterman, A. S. (1992). Identity as an aspect of optimal psychological functioning. In G. R. Adams, T. P. Gullotta, & R. Montemayor (Eds.), *Adolescent identity formation* (pp. 50–72). Newbury Park, CA: Sage.

Wayment, H. A., Wiist, B., Sullivan, B. M., & Warren, M. A. (2011). Doing and being: Mindfulness, health, and quiet ego characteristics among Buddhist practitioners. *Journal of Happiness Studies, 12*(4), 575–589.

Weinstein, N., Brown, K. W., & Ryan, R. M. (2009). A multi-method examination of the effects of mindfulness on stress attribution, coping, and emotional well-being. *Journal of Research in Personality, 43,* 374–385.

Weissberg, R. P., Walberg, H. J., O'Brien, M. U., & Kuster, C. B. (Eds.). (2003). *Long-term trends in the well-being of children and youth.* Washington, DC: Child Welfare League of America Press.

Welwood, J. (1996). *Love and awakening.* New York: HarperCollins.

Willard, C. (2010). *Child's mind: Mindfulness practices to help our children be more focused, calm, and relaxed.* Berkeley, CA: Parallax Press.

Williams, M., & Penman, D. (2011). *Mindfulness: An eight-week plan for finding peace in a frantic world.* New York: Rodale.

Wilson, J. (2014). *Mindful America: The mutual transformation of Buddhist meditation and American culture.* New York: Oxford University Press.

Wood, D. (2005). *The secret of saying thanks.* New York: Simon & Schuster.

# INDEX

# Y

# Z

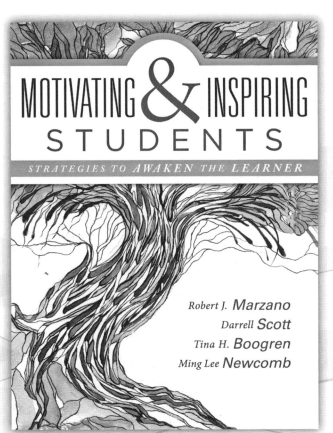

# Unleash the power of mindfulness in classrooms

 Signature PD Service

## Cultivating Mindfulness in Schools Workshop

Providing students with the tools of mindfulness has the potential to improve their self-concept, interpersonal relationships, academic achievement, and mental and physical health. Gain an understanding of the research that supports integrating mindfulness in schools and explore practical tools and strategies for incorporating mindfulness activities in classrooms.

- Understand five major benefits of mindfulness: stress reduction, attention, emotional control, positive self-concept, and positive interactions.
- Gain an understanding of the importance of modeling, teaching, and reinforcing mindfulness.
- Discover practical activities to help students develop a positive self-concept and improve their overall well-being.
- Explore useful tools for helping students focus their attention, reduce stress, and bring awareness to their emotions.
- Learn ways to educate school leaders, parents, and students as to the need for mindfulness in the classroom and schools.

# Learn more!
MarzanoResearch.com/CMCPD